I0820938

Jean Fischer

Living Water

Devotional Refreshment for a Woman's Soul

Print ISBN 979-8-89151-089-0

Published by Barbour Publishing, Inc., 1810 Barbour Drive, Uhrichsville, Ohio 44683, www.barbourbooks.com

Our mission is to inspire the world with the life-changing message of the Bible.

Printed in China.

Jesus answered,
"If you knew the
generosity of God
and who I am,
you would be
asking me for a drink,
and I would give you fresh,
living water."

John 4:10 MSG

Introduction

As water acts as a mirror to a face, so the heart of man acts as a mirror to a man.
PROVERBS 27:19

If you look at your reflection in the water, it won't be perfectly clear. The water distorts your image. It will never be as perfect as an altered photograph that wipes away the flaws. The image looking back at you is a reflection of how you appear to God. We are imperfect human beings created by Him and deeply loved by Him in spite of our imperfections. No matter how hard we try, our reflection won't be made perfect unless we accept the fact that Jesus died to take away our sins so our hearts will be ready for heaven. Jesus is the source of "living water." It means He sustains us spiritually by showing us the truth of God's Word. His gift of salvation allows us full access to God, the Holy Spirit, and eventually heaven. When we accept Him as Savior, we will never again be thirsty for comfort, rest, or peace. Jesus walks with us through the valleys and leads us to the mountaintop. He will never leave us alone. We can imagine Him speaking to us today saying, "Come. Drink the living water. Drink from the well that never runs dry."

Rivers of Living Water

As the deer desires rivers of water,
so my soul desires You, O God.
PSALM 42:1

In Psalm 42, a troubled King David cries out, "My soul is thirsty for God, for the living God" (verse 2). We don't know where David was when he wrote Psalm 42, but imagine him sitting on a riverbank in a quiet, secluded place alone with God. While he prays, David notices a deer drinking from the flowing river. "As the deer desires rivers of water, so my soul desires You, O God," David says. He is in a rough spot in life. David longs for how things used to be. Still, he puts his hope in God for better days ahead. He says, "The Lord will send His loving-kindness in the day. And His song will be with me in the night" (verse 8).

Maybe, like David, you are experiencing a stress-filled, unhappy time. Find a quiet place to be alone with Jesus. Listen as He says, "If anyone is thirsty, let him come to Me and drink. . . . Rivers of living water will flow from the heart of the one who puts his trust in Me" (John 7:37–38). Pray and remind yourself that Jesus is trustworthy. He will pour His Holy Spirit into you like a rushing river of hope and lead you to better days.

Jesus, You alone are my safe place. Pour a river of hope into my heart as I put my trust in You.

First Things First

Seek first God's kingdom and what God wants.
Then all your other needs will be met as well.
MATTHEW 6:33 NCV

How do you begin your day? If you are a busy wife and mom, you probably wake up early, get yourself ready, and then turn your attention to sending your kids off to school. During those first hours in the morning, your mind floods with to-dos—thoughts about your workday, errands to be run, a meeting to attend, a check-in with your elderly parents, a doctor's appointment. . . You kiss your husband goodbye, make sure he hasn't forgotten anything he needs, and remind him of *his* to-do list.

A busy schedule combined with a cluttered mind leaves little room for the Lord. In Matthew 6:33, Jesus tells us to put God first. Make Him your first priority in the morning. Before things get crazy-busy, spend time with Him. Begin your day with prayer. Ask God to lead you through the day according to His will. And don't stop there. Talk with Him on your way to work, at work, while you run errands, as you wait for your appointments, and throughout the day. God is faithful. When you put Him first in your heart, He will meet your every need.

Good morning, Father. I give this day to You. Lead me through it and meet my needs according to Your will.

Lost for Words

When you are put into their hands, do not worry what you will say or how you will say it. The words will be given you when the time comes. It will not be you who will speak the words. The Spirit of your Father will speak through you.

MATTHEW 10:19–20

Whether it's interviewing for a job, consoling a hurting friend, working through a disagreement, or even going on a first date, we get the jitters worrying about the right things to say. Our hearts race as we imagine what could happen. We think about what we should say and shouldn't say. Rehearsing the conversation in our minds, we put words together and imagine how they might be received and the impression they will make.

Jesus had this advice for His disciples: "Do not worry what you will say or how you will say it. The words will be given you when the time comes." Jesus said the Holy Spirit would help them. His advice is for you too. When you don't know what to say, be quick to listen and slow to speak. Ask the Holy Spirit to guide you. Listen to the Spirit of your heavenly Father as He speaks the right words into your heart at the right time. Trust Him to help and direct you.

Holy Spirit, I am at a loss for words. You know the circumstances. Give me the words You want me to say.

Leave the Light On

The Lord is my light and the One Who saves me.
Whom should I fear? The Lord is the strength
of my life. Of whom should I be afraid?
Psalm 27:1

"Mommy, please leave the light on." Does that sound like your little one when you tuck him or her into bed? Most young children go through a phase when they are afraid of the dark. It isn't so much fear of darkness as fear of what might be lurking there, what is unseen. Imaginations run wild. What is that noise? Whose shadow is that in the corner? Is there a monster under my bed? Light in the room makes the darkness less scary.

Grown-ups are afraid of the dark too. Anxiety and worry create a spiritual darkness inside our hearts. Fear of the unseen separates us from God, and we imagine scary things lurking ahead. The good news is spiritual darkness is no match for the light of God. He always leaves the light on. In the Bible, John writes that Jesus has existed forever as the Light of the World. The darkness has never been able to put out His light (John 1:1–5). The light of Jesus keeps us focused on Him instead of our fears. When you lie down to sleep and worries fill your head, just tell Him, "Jesus, please leave the light on."

Lord Jesus, calm my fears. Fill my heart with the light of Your love.

The King's Daughter

"I will be a Father to you. You will be My sons and daughters, says the All-powerful God."
2 CORINTHIANS 6:18

When you were little, did you want to be a princess? Princesses are everywhere these days, at theme parks, at birthday parties, in movies, and on TV. Little girls are obsessed with them, probably because they are everywhere but more so because princesses live charmed lives. As kings' daughters, they are entitled to everything in the kingdom—beautiful clothes, gourmet meals, expensive jewelry, a stylist for perfect makeup and hair, and (of course) a perfect Prince Charming. Maybe you still wish you could be a princess. But behind the façade of perfection, just like everyone else, princesses can't escape life's perils. Nothing in the kingdom, not even the king, can remove a princess' anxiety, sadness, or fear. But there is one King who can—our all-powerful God, King of all the earth (Psalm 47:7). You are His daughter. He will bring you through life's troubles and take away your sadness and fear. God can turn around any situation. So embrace your identity as His princess. God made you. He chose you, and He loves you. You have access to Him 24-7. You are blessed, forgiven, and entitled to all His kingdom has to offer, now and forever!

Heavenly Father, with a grateful heart, I thank You for making me Your daughter, meeting all my needs, and providing an eternal home for me in Your kingdom.

A Dry Spell

"The Lord will always lead you. He will meet the needs of your soul in the dry times and give strength to your body. You will be like a garden that has enough water, like a well of water that never dries up."

Isaiah 58:11

Imagine the frustration die-hard gardeners face living in hot climates with watering restrictions. In some places during a dry spell, it's the law to water just one day a week. Twelve minutes are allowed for watering grass. Plants and trees are allowed water just once every seven to fourteen days. Verdant, perfectly manicured lawns deteriorate to straw, tender plants languish, and new trees beg for a longer, deeper drink. There's not much a gardener can do but pray for rain.

Our souls go through dry times too. We traverse a spiritual desert where everything goes wrong and solutions to problems dry up. We grow weary and want our souls renewed. We seek refreshment. Isaiah 58:11 reminds us there is an oasis in the desert—it's Jesus! When we pray and ask Him to lead us, He will bring us to His well of living water that never dries up. Jesus promises to meet our every need until we become like well-watered gardens, roots quenched, each tender leaf and delicate flower satisfied and strong.

Lord Jesus, I feel weary and lost. Lead me to the well of Your living water. Refresh my tired soul and renew my strength.

Persistent Prayer

"O Lord God! See, You have made the heavens and the earth by Your great power and by Your long arm! Nothing is too hard for You!"
JEREMIAH 32:17

Some who have gone through a near-death experience say they saw prayers ascending to heaven in a whirlwind. Bold, desperate prayers; fervent and persistent prayers. Prayers for relief from financial troubles, problems at work, and relationship issues. Prayers for salvation for a family member, for sickness to be healed, for children gone astray, for those in service risking their lives. . .so many prayers.

What are you praying for? What is that one request you persistently bring to God day after day? Prayer is more than just asking. It is asking continuously. It requires waiting and trusting that God will answer. When waiting is hard, it helps to remember God's greatness. He spoke the heavens and earth into existence. He knows the number of stars and calls each by name. Nothing is too hard for our all-powerful God. You can be sure He will answer your prayers in His own time and way. "'Test me in this,' says the LORD Almighty, 'and see if I will not throw open the floodgates of heaven and pour out so much blessing that there will not be room enough to store it'" (Malachi 3:10 NIV).

Lord God, no force in heaven or on earth is more powerful than You. I will be patient, believing You will answer my prayers.

Off to See the Wizard

It is better to trust in the Lord than to trust in man.

PSALM 118:8

In the film *The Wizard of Oz*, Dorothy and her friends each lack something important. Dorothy wants to return home to Kansas, the Tin Woodman longs for a heart, the Scarecrow wishes he had a brain, and the Lion desires courage. The friends travel to Emerald City to find the Great and Powerful Oz, the one who can make anything happen, or so they believe. They soon discover Oz is just a man behind a curtain, powerless to do the impossible. Their misplaced faith led them. . .nowhere.

Psalm 118:8 warns about putting too much faith and trust in people. As much as others might want to help us, humans can't meet our every need. Jesus said, "Have faith in God. For sure, I tell you, a person may say to this mountain, 'Move from here into the sea.' And if he does not doubt, but believes that what he says will be done, it will happen" (Mark 11:22–23). Of course, we can't literally move mountains into the sea. But when we put our faith in God, we know He can remove the mountains in life that get in our way. He gives us confidence to overcome even the most difficult situations.

Oh God, I trust You. If You plan to move this mountain, it will move!

Our Generous God

"Would any of you fathers give your son a stone if he asked for bread? Or would you give a snake if he asked for a fish? . . . You are sinful and you know how to give good things to your children. How much more will your Father in heaven give the Holy Spirit to those who ask Him?"

LUKE 11:11, 13

As moms, we want the best for our children. We willingly, even joyfully, sacrifice our wants and needs for their well-being and happiness. Whether it means working two jobs to make ends meet or working fewer hours so we can spend more time with our kids, we generously provide what they need.

In Luke 11, Jesus reminds us of God's abundant generosity. Our heavenly Father knows our needs as well as the needs of our children. He desires to provide beyond our greatest expectations. When we ask for God's help, He consistently and generously pours the Holy Spirit into our souls to guide, comfort, strengthen, and even pray for us. What we want isn't necessarily what we need. So when we pray, we should ask God to guide us according to His will and to open our eyes to His blessings. When we look for His blessings in our lives, then we become even more aware of His generosity.

Heavenly Father, I praise You for Your generosity. Provide my family with everything we need. Bless us abundantly according to Your will.

Overpacked and Overburdened

"For My way of carrying a load
is easy and My load is not heavy."
MATTHEW 11:30

Air travel can be a stressful experience, especially when you have multiple heavy bags. Imagine this: You are alone outside the airport. Your Uber driver dropped you off curbside. He unloaded your luggage from his van and drove off. Usually, you find luggage carts nearby, but not today. You look for a porter to help carry your bags, but none is in sight. You are already running late. Frantically, you look for a way to solve your problem and then Jesus shows up—yes, Jesus! He says, "Let Me carry those for you." You think, *I can't possibly allow Jesus, the one who has done so much for me already, to carry this load. It's mine to deal with. I'll figure it out.*

Too often, we carry life's burdens by ourselves. We look for solutions and find none. All the while, Jesus says to us, "Let Me carry that for you." Still, when we hear Him, we remain fiercely independent, reluctant to give Him our troubles, convinced we can find our own way. Jesus wants to carry our baggage. He wants us to unburden ourselves so He can take control and help. Are you carrying a heavy load? Give it to Jesus. What seems so heavy to you is to Him featherlight.

Jesus, I surrender to You everything that is weighing me down. Please take this heavy load and help me.

Get Going!

But Moses said, "O Lord, I ask of You,
send some other person."
EXODUS 4:13

Egypt's pharaoh held the Israelites captive as slaves, and God planned to get them out. He went to Moses and said, "I am sending you to Pharaoh to bring my people the Israelites out of Egypt" (Exodus 3:10 NIV). Moses wasn't the most confident of men. His thoughts overflowed with everything that could go wrong. *No way, I can't do that!* he thought. "Please, God," Moses said, "send someone else." God knew, given the chance, Moses had the potential to become a great leader. "Please send someone else," Moses begged. "What if they won't believe me or listen to me?" God wouldn't let Moses off that easily. He said to him, "Get going." God sent Moses to Egypt, and He didn't send him alone. He allowed Moses to take his brother Aaron along for support.

God knows your potential too. Where you lack confidence, He will nudge you outside your comfort zone. He says, "I will teach you what you are to do" (Exodus 4:15). When you agree to His plans, you can count on God to send others to help and support you. Do you sense Him leading you to do something important? Don't be afraid. Take His hand. Get going.

I accept Your challenge, God. I will do what You ask, knowing it will build confidence in myself and in You.

This Is Your Time

"And who knows but that you have come to your royal position for such a time as this?"

Esther 4:14 NIV

Esther won a beauty contest to become the wife of Ahasuerus, Persia's king. Esther hid her true identity from the king. Entering the contest, she was a Jew pretending to be Persian. (Jews lived in Persia, but they were not welcome there.) Haman, a high-ranking official in the kingdom, hated Esther's relative Mordecai, because Mordecai, a Jew, refused to bow to him. Haman convinced the king to have Mordecai and all the Jews in the kingdom murdered. When Mordecai found out, he begged Esther to tell the king. "Who knows," he said, "but that you have come to your royal position for such a time as this?" Esther risked her life telling the king she was a Jew and asking him to save her people. Her story ends with the Jews saved, the king still in love with her, and Mordecai made the highest-ranking official in the kingdom.

Although God is never mentioned in Esther's Bible story, He had her exactly where He wanted her in His plan to save the Jews. God has you exactly where He wants you too. You might not know how you fit into His plan, but you can be sure He has a purpose for you being right here, right now.

Father, thank You for whatever purpose You have planned for me. It is my honor to serve You.

The Compost Pile

God made my life complete when I placed all the pieces before him.
2 Samuel 22:21 MSG

Composting is the process of recycling food scraps, leaves, and yard trimmings. Its purpose is to create nutrient-rich compost that can be mixed into garden soil. Gardeners create compost piles by layering yard and food wastes and allowing them to decompose. It can take anywhere from several weeks to a year for the scraps to disintegrate. It's a process requiring patience and diligence, tending and turning the pile regularly, adding water, mixing greens and browns. . . The goal is to get the pile to "cook" and thoroughly break down. Those new to the process often have trouble getting it right. But if they rely on advice from seasoned gardeners who know whether the pile is too wet, too dry, too small, or off-balance, their compost piles produce robust, nutrient-rich soil and beautiful gardens.

Our lives are like compost piles. If by ourselves we try to break down our messes and make them into something good, we fail. But if we listen to God, the gardener, and rely on His advice, He can turn our messes into miracles. No mess is too messy for God. Give your mess to Him today. Ask Him to tend it, mend it, and turn it into something beautiful.

Lord, I've made a mess of things. Help me. Guide me, and by Your grace turn my mess into a blessing.

Something's Happening Here

Do not conform to the pattern of this world, but be transformed by the renewing of your mind. Then you will be able to test and approve what God's will is—his good, pleasing and perfect will.

ROMANS 12:2 NIV

The 1960s were tumultuous years in America. Opinions ran strong and divided about what was right and wrong. During this decade, the songwriter and musician Stephen Stills penned the lyrics to the popular song "For What It's Worth." The song reflected the changes taking place in the country. The sixties was a counterculture era when conventional mores were tested and rejected.

We live in a similar time of unrest and confusion. What's happening and what's right or wrong isn't always clear. Romans 12:2 tells us not to conform to the pattern of the world but instead to agree with God's ideas of what is good, pleasing, and perfect. The Bible is our guide. When we read it, meditate on its words, and hold them inside our hearts, then we can discern right from wrong. If we are unsure, we can ask for wisdom. The Bible says, "If any of you lacks wisdom, you should ask God, who gives generously to all without finding fault, and it will be given to you" (James 1:5 NIV). God is ready to give abundant wisdom to all who ask.

Heavenly Father, teach me. Make clear any false ideas I have about what is right or wrong.

Free Fall

"When you pass through the waters, I will be with you. When you pass through the rivers, they will not flow over you. When you walk through the fire, you will not be burned. The fire will not destroy you. For I am the Lord your God, the Holy One of Israel, Who saves you."

ISAIAH 43:2–3

Ten-year-old Christina finally felt brave enough to ride the **roller** coaster. She climbed into the seat next to her mother and put on the safety restraint. Slowly, the car moved up toward the sky. Christina enjoyed the ride until the car rounded the top and went into a free fall. Christina's stomach dropped. Her heart raced with fear as she felt herself falling, falling. . . In desperation, she grabbed her mother's hand, held it tight, and wanted nothing else but the ride to end.

Life is a roller coaster. It's fun until it sends you spiraling downward, making you feel out of control. When the gravity of a situation hurls you into a free fall, God says to hold on to Him until the ride is over. He will comfort and protect you. Whatever fears you face today, know that God is along for the ride. You can trust Him to bring you through it and set your feet on solid ground.

Lord God, when I am afraid, You are my shelter and my strength. I will put my trust in You.

The Big Fail

It is because of the Lord's loving-kindness that we are not destroyed for His loving-pity never ends. It is new every morning. He is so very faithful.

LAMENTATIONS 3:22–23

Some of the most common recurring dreams are about failure. Maybe you have dreamed you are failing at your job or that you are singing at your sister's wedding and everyone is laughing at you. We dream about failure because we know how it feels and we fear it. Failure hurts. It's embarrassing. We care what people think of us, and we want to be accepted, liked, and loved.

How we deal with failure is more important than how people react when we fail. We can let failure (or fear of it) ruin our lives, or we can view each morning as a fresh start. Allowing defeat to define us leads to fear and low self-esteem. It sets us up to fail. But each new day, God gives us a gift, a do-over—an opportunity to forgive ourselves, to let go of our failures, and to try again. God knows we aren't perfect; He expects us to fail. And when we do, God is there to pick up the pieces and give us another chance. Isn't it wonderful knowing God's loving-kindness transcends our failures?

Lord God, I need You. Help me to overcome my fear of failing. Give me the courage to put my failures behind me and the confidence to try again.

True Joy

I receive joy when I am weak. I receive joy when people talk against me and make it hard for me and try to hurt me and make trouble for me. I receive joy when all these things come to me because of Christ. For when I am weak, then I am strong.

2 CORINTHIANS 12:10

The apostle Paul had a tough life. He said, "I've. . .been jailed. . .beaten up. . .at death's door. . .flogged. . .pummeled with rocks. . .shipwrecked three times. . .had to ford rivers, fend off robbers, struggle with friends, struggle with foes. . .[been] betrayed by those I thought were my brothers. . .[known] many a long and lonely night without sleep, many a missed meal, blasted by the cold, naked to the weather. And that's not the half of it, when you throw in the daily pressures and anxieties of all the churches" (2 Corinthians 11:23–29 MSG). Wow, what a list! Still, through all his trials Paul found joy because he knew Jesus was with him, helping and strengthening him. True joy, Paul's kind of joy, comes from finding strength in Jesus, trusting in His help and protection, and resting in His love. Do you know that kind of joy?

Dear Jesus, fill my heart with the kind of joy that comes from knowing and trusting in You.

When God Is Silent

Who put wisdom inside the mind or understanding in the heart? Who has the wisdom to count the clouds? Who can pour water from the jars of the sky when the dust becomes hard and the clumps of dirt stick together?

JOB 38:36–38 NCV

Are you in a season when God seems distant? We all experience times when God withholds something we've asked for. It could be healing for a broken heart, a sick body, a severed relationship. . . We pray, we ask, and nothing changes. In our frustration, we cry out, "God, where are You?" We might even doubt whether God exists or whether He can fix what is broken.

Job was in such a season. He wondered why God was silent, why his prayers for relief seemed to fall on deaf ears, and why God seemed far away. *Why, why, why?* After listening to Job's list of questions, God responded with some questions of His own, starting with "Where were you when I made the earth's foundation?" (Job 38:4 NCV). Instead of answering Job's whys, God reminded Job to look around and notice God's power everywhere.

If you doubt God can or will help you, instead of dwelling on the whys, concentrate on who! Look up. Our all-powerful God can and will heal your hurts and lead you out of trouble.

Oh God, remind me that even when You are silent, You love me and will never leave me.

God's Contact List

Your eyes saw me before I was put together.
And all the days of my life were written in Your book before any of them came to be.

Psalm 139:16

Your smartphone is your camera, media player, GPS, and handheld computer, but most importantly it's the way you connect with family, friends, and others. If you're like most women, the contact list on your phone is long. It includes names, addresses, phone numbers, emails, and everything you need to connect using a simple tap or click.

God has a contact list too. It's called the Book of Life. God wrote down all the days of your life even before He created the universe. In His book, He also records the names of those who accept Jesus as Lord and Savior. Everyone's name is in the book, but you can imagine checkmarks next to the names of those who put their trust in Jesus. If your name has a checkmark, you get to spend eternity in the presence of your Savior. Jesus promised nothing would ever remove your name from the list. In heaven, He will present to God and His angels all those whose names are written there (Revelation 3:5). Is there a checkmark next to your name in God's Book of Life? The line to heaven is always open, and God is ready to take your call.

I'm grateful, Lord God, that my name is on Your contact list. I'm grateful too that You want me to live with You in heaven.

Growing Pains

"Why do You hide Your face, and think of me as one who hates You?"

JOB 13:24

"You just don't get it. You don't understand! Why do you hate me?" If that sounds like your teenager, you're not alone. The teen years are especially difficult when the desire to be independent leads to frustration and even rebellion. Parents struggle with not giving in to what their children want, and kids find it impossible to believe their parents know what's best.

Our heavenly Father is a parent to rebellious kids of all ages, even adults. None of us is guiltless. At some point, we have been angry or frustrated with God for not giving us what we wanted. It's impossible to understand His ways and easy to think we know better than He does. When we grow and mature as Christians, it becomes clearer why God said no to what we asked for. Likewise, as our children grow and mature, they look back at our decisions and understand we did what was best. If you are riding the waves of your teen's emotions, be patient and reach out to God. Stay strong. Love your child unconditionally and pray constantly for him or her. Ask God to give you wisdom to guide your child to adulthood.

Father God, please help me parent my teenagers. Help me to be patient and strong and to make wise decisions. Watch over my children and lead them in the way they should go.

And Then That Happened!

Trust in the Lord with all your heart, and do not trust in your own understanding. Agree with Him in all your ways, and He will make your paths straight.

PROVERBS 3:5–6

Life was going along smoothly, and then *that* happened! An accident, illness, job loss, fractured relationship. . . *That* happened, and it rocked your world. The unexpected twists and turns in life throw us off course. We want to know what's coming so we can plan. We want our paths straight with no surprises. But life isn't like that. We don't know what will happen, why it will happen, or how it will affect us. And that makes us feel anxious.

Read the Bible and you will find its people facing all kinds of twists and turns. They struggled to find their way until God helped them. When they finally put their trust in Him, He led them down a path straight and narrow. God will do that for you too. The key is trust. When something unexpected happens, when you realize you aren't in control and you panic, ask God to calm you. Ask Him to give you confidence and lead you. Then trust that He will! Memorize Proverbs 3:5–6. Make it your go-to verse when the unexpected happens.

Oh God! I can't believe that happened. I trust You to help me, calm me, and give me strength. Lead me in the way I should go.

Blurred Vision

*"Stop judging by mere appearances,
but instead judge correctly."*
JOHN 7:24 NIV

God gave Samuel the task of appointing a new king of Israel. He said to Samuel, "You must appoint the one I show you" (1 Samuel 16:3 NCV). God said the new king would be among the sons of Jesse. So Samuel went to see Jesse. He met seven of Jesse's strong, handsome sons; and with each, Samuel thought, *This is the one.* But God said, "Do not look at the way he looks on the outside or how tall he is, because I have not chosen him. For the Lord does not look at the things man looks at. A man looks at the outside of a person, but the Lord looks at the heart" (1 Samuel 16:7). Samuel asked Jesse, "Do you have more sons?" Jesse answered there was his youngest son, David. Jesse hadn't thought to include him because anyone who looked at David would see he was just a boy, a small shepherd boy. To Samuel's surprise, God said, "This is the one."

There is more to a person than meets the eye. God wants us to see like He does, to look beyond what's on the outside and into a person's heart. If we do, we might be surprised by what we see.

Lord, I am guilty of sometimes judging people by their appearance. Help me to see them through Your eyes and discover what's inside their hearts.

Rose-Colored Glasses

The wise see danger ahead and avoid it,
but fools keep going and get into trouble.
PROVERBS 27:12 NCV

Do you view life through rose-colored glasses? It's not a bad thing to find good in every situation. God's blessings are all around us, and seeing them, even in difficult times, is a character trait worth having. A positive view of life makes us more aware of and thankful for God's loving-kindness. But there is another connotation to looking at life through rose-colored lenses. It can mean ignoring reality and not seeing its potential danger or risks.

Proverbs 27:12 reminds us to open our eyes to the reality of evil and avoid it. Some versions of the Bible say to hide from evil or to take cover. Evil is not something to take lightly. John says, in 1 John 4:1, "Dear Christian friends, do not believe every spirit. But test the spirits to see if they are from God for there are many false preachers in the world." And not just false preachers, but false practices, ideas, teachings. . . We tell our children, "Be careful—that might hurt you!" God says the same to us. Study the Bible. Open your eyes to evil and avoid it. Then be wise and stay out of trouble.

Heavenly Father, I will run from evil and hide in the truth of Your Word. Give me eyes to discern evil and wisdom to avoid it.

Earthquake

The people asked him, "Then what should we do?" He answered them, "If you have two coats, give one to him who has none. If you have food, you must share some."

LUKE 3:10–11

They felt a quick jolt. The earth rolled and shook, objects moved across the floor, and bookcases fell, spilling their contents. The sound of glass shattering mingled with an ominous rumbling. Walls and buildings fell, and then there was fire. This is what the citizens of San Francisco experienced in the great earthquake of 1906. Everything around them was pushed down and shaken together. As they stood helpless among the rubble, others hurried to assist. They gave whatever they had—time, effort, food, clothing—expecting nothing in return.

Whatever "earthquakes" we experience in life, whether a divorce, the death of a loved one, an illness, or financial trouble, we can count on God to send people to help. Jesus commanded us to help one another. He says in Luke 6:38, "Give, and it will be given to you. You will have more than enough. It can be pushed down and shaken together and it will still run over as it is given to you. The way you give to others is the way you will receive in return."

Is there someone you can help today? Ask God to guide you.

Lord God, when I've had trouble, You've sent people to help me. Lead me now to give back and be a helper to those in need.

Yes, I Can!

I can do all things because Christ gives me the strength.
PHILIPPIANS 4:13

The television show *Life Below Zero* follows a series of individuals who reside in remote areas of Alaska. They live off the land, battling known and unknown challenges that come with life in the wilderness.

One of them is Sue Aikens, owner of Kavik River Camp,[1] fifteen miles from the Arctic Ocean. The closest road is eighty miles away. The nearest big city is Fairbanks, five hundred miles from Kavik. Sue hosts visitors at the camp from June through September. The rest of the year she lives there alone. She hunts and fishes for her food, maintains the camp and its small airstrip, and braves the dangers of subzero temperatures, heavy snow, and grizzly bears and other predators. She thrives on being alone, relishing the freedom, challenging herself, and succeeding beyond her expectations.

Maybe there is something big and exciting you want to do, but you think you aren't good enough, strong enough, or smart enough. Don't let that stop you. The first step is saying, "Yes, I can!" If your dream aligns with God's will, He will provide everything you need to succeed. Talk with Him about your dreams. Go where He leads you. Get ready to be amazed by what you will accomplish.

Lord, I'm worried my dream is bigger than my determination and strength. I'm afraid to take the first step. Let's talk about it. What should I do?

The Good, the Bad, the Ugly

Christian brothers, keep your minds thinking about whatever is true, whatever is respected, whatever is right, whatever is pure, whatever can be loved, and whatever is well thought of. If there is anything good and worth giving thanks for, think about these things.

PHILIPPIANS 4:8

What are you thinking about today? Do those thoughts make you feel worried, anxious, angry, afraid? The thoughts we allow into our heads affect how we feel. There is a spiritual tug-of-war going on. Satan wants to fill our minds with negative, bad, ugly thoughts. God wants us to remember that no matter what is bothering us today, He already has it worked out for our good.

In today's Bible verse, Paul tells us to keep our thoughts centered on godly things. It's easier said than done. Negative thoughts have a way of slipping in unnoticed. It takes practice to recognize them and turn them around. Paul says, "We break down every thought and proud thing that puts itself up against the wisdom of God. We take hold of every thought and make it obey Christ" (2 Corinthians 10:5). Take a few minutes right now to name something true, respected, right, pure, and something or someone you love. Get in the habit of thinking good thoughts every day.

Jesus, help me to set my thoughts on You and to give thanks for what is true, respected, right, pure, and loved.

Off Course

"My people have been lost sheep; their shepherds have led them astray and caused them to roam on the mountains. They wandered over mountain and hill and forgot their own resting place."

JEREMIAH 50:6 NIV

The GPS in cars and phones is a useful tool—until it's not. Technology isn't perfect. A GPS might not alert about a detour or road construction. It can show our location incorrectly, setting us miles from where we are. Its directions can be inaccurate, and sometimes it doesn't work at all. When the GPS fails, we rely on our own judgment. We turn where we think we should, and before long we're wandering a long, lonely road, going in circles, lost.

Something similar happened to the Israelites when they traveled to the Promised Land. Obviously, they didn't have a GPS. But they had something better—God! He knew the way. If they had listened, trusted Him, and relied on His directions, they wouldn't have spent forty years wandering in the desert. They didn't listen. They made wrong turns and got lost.

God is not like your GPS. His directions are perfect all the time. Whenever you feel lost, He knows the way home. So before you panic and make a wrong turn, pull off the road and ask God for directions. He will never lead you off course.

Father God, wherever I go, You are ahead of me. Remind me to follow You.

Cravings

As new babies want milk, you should want to drink the pure milk which is God's Word so you will grow up and be saved from the punishment of sin.

1 PETER 2:2

Merriam-Webster defines a craving as "an intense, urgent, or abnormal desire or longing."[2] A popular fast-food restaurant offers a "cravings" menu: crunchy tacos with your choice of fillings, burritos stuffed with beef and beans, loaded nachos topped with a generous dollop of sour cream. . . Is your mouth watering yet? The mere suggestion of certain foods increases our cravings—salty chips, a chocolate-glazed donut, a juicy burger oozing with cheese, an ice-cold drink on a hot day. As we learn, grow, and try new things, we develop new cravings. Some are good. Others are not.

There is only one food newborn babies crave: pure milk. A mother's milk provides the best nutrition for growth and development. It contains antibodies to help boost immunity and fight infection. In today's scripture, Peter compares the Bible to the pure "milk" that is God's Word. He says we should desire it because it's necessary for our spiritual growth and development. It helps us fight the bad cravings that infiltrate our souls. Psalm 34:8 says, "O taste and see that the Lord is good." The more we drink of God's spiritual "milk," the more we crave and thirst for it.

Oh Lord, increase my desire for Your Word.
Lead me to crave it night and day.

When Forgiveness Is Hard

Then Jesus said, "Father, forgive them.
They do not know what they are doing."
LUKE 23:34

Has someone hurt you so badly that you find it impossible to forgive him or her? The Bible says you must, but your heart says, "I can't!" You're human, after all. You are a human with feelings running deep and raw.

Jesus was falsely accused, judged, found guilty, beaten, mocked, shamed, spit upon, humiliated, and nailed to a cross. He suffered excruciating, unbearable pain while nailed there, and then He experienced intense loneliness separated from God while He accepted the punishment we deserve for our sins. Yet, while enduring all that, Jesus said, "Father, forgive them. They do not know what they are doing."

For Christians, Jesus is our role model, and our ultimate goal is to become more like Him. Jesus taught us to forgive. Peter asked how many times he must forgive someone, and Jesus answered, "Seventy times seven" (Matthew 18:21–22). If we find forgiveness impossible, we can turn our thoughts to Jesus, His suffering, and His willingness to forgive. We can ask Him to help with our unforgiveness. Forgiving someone doesn't mean forgetting or saying something is okay. Instead, it's surrendering the hurt to Jesus and working at becoming more like Him. In doing so, we can heal and find peace.

Dear Jesus, please teach me to be forgiving like You are. Take my hurt and anger and help me to heal.

And If Not. . .

"But even if He does not, we want you to know,
O king, that we will not serve your gods or worship
the object of gold that you have set up."
DANIEL 3:18

King Nebuchadnezzar had appointed Shadrach, Meshach, and Abednego as leaders over the land of Babylon. One day, the king's spokesman announced, "This is what you must do, O people of every nation and language: When you hear the sound of. . .all kinds of music, you are to get down on your knees and worship the object of gold that King Nebuchadnezzar has set up. Whoever does not get down and worship will be thrown at once into the big and hot fire" (Daniel 3:4–6). Shadrach, Meshach, and Abednego served God. They refused to bow to the king's gold statue. They told the king, "If we are thrown into the fire, our God Whom we serve is able to save us from it" (verse 17). They said even if God did not save them, they would remain faithful to Him.

Shadrach, Meshach, and Abednego's story brought about a popular contemporary saying: And if not, He is still good. True faith means remaining committed to God and believing He is still good even when He doesn't rescue us from evil or danger the way we hope. Do you have that kind of faith?

Lord God, strengthen my faith so even if my life is in danger, all I see is Your goodness.

First Steps

"For I am the Lord your God Who holds your right hand, and Who says to you, 'Do not be afraid. I will help you.'"

ISAIAH 41:13

Parents ooh and aah and celebrate their babies' first steps. But for babies, those steps are uncertain, maybe even a little scary. When their world looks different from that new perspective, we take our babies' hands and say, "Don't be afraid. I'll help you." New toddlers are unsteady in their walk. Sometimes they fall. Sometimes they cry. But Mom and Dad are there to hold them up, comfort them, and give them confidence to try again.

Sometimes we forget that God is our Father. He is the best daddy we could ever ask for. Whenever we are unsure of taking the first step or whenever we fall, He takes our hand and tells us, "Don't be afraid. I'll help you." The author of Psalm 94 (most likely David) says, "When I said, 'My foot is going out from under me,' Your loving-kindness held me up, O Lord. When my worry is great within me, Your comfort brings joy to my soul" (verses 18–19). Our heavenly Father's hand is gentle but firm. His loving-kindness will hold you up. Take His hand today and start walking. Then keep walking, confident and unafraid.

Kind heavenly Father, I'm afraid to take that first step. Take my hand. Hold me up and help me.

Doom Mongers

How happy are the people who know the sound of joy! They walk in the light of Your face, O Lord. They are full of joy in Your name all day long. And by being right with You, they are honored.

Psalm 89:15–16

Doom monger: "someone who tries to make people believe that something very bad is going to happen, usually when this is not necessary or reasonable."[3] Do you know a doom monger? It could be someone you work with, a family member, a friend, or even you! When we get caught up in the pessimism surrounding us, it leads to hopelessness and self-pity.

The actress Rachel Dratch tells of being on vacation in Costa Rica when someone asked her, "Where are you from?" When she answered, "New York," the doom monger steered the conversation to the most horrific events of 9/11. This gave Rachel the idea to create a comedy persona for her character on a popular television show, a character whose constant doom-mongering would make people laugh.[4]

The best way to handle doom mongers is to turn the conversation toward something good. God is good all the time. Evidence of His goodness is everywhere, and that gives us hope. Focusing on Him, His power, and His blessings is the best way to turn pessimism into joy.

Guard my heart, Lord, from the negativity that surrounds me. Lead me to share a positive attitude and bring happiness into the world.

Get Behind Me, Satan!

Submit yourselves, then, to God.
Resist the devil, and he will flee from you.
JAMES 4:7 NIV

James said if we resist Satan, he will leave us. In what ways can we resist? In Matthew 4:1–11 Satan tempts Jesus to sin. With each temptation, Jesus responds with scripture. This teaches us that using God's truths and promises from the Bible is one way to resist. Ephesians 6:11 says we can resist by putting on an "armor" made of God's truth, righteousness, the gospel, faith, our salvation, and the power of the Holy Spirit. The evangelist Oswald Chambers offered yet another idea based on Colossians 3:5 (NIV), where Paul says, "Put to death, therefore, whatever belongs to your earthly nature: sexual immorality, impurity, lust, evil desires and greed, which is idolatry." Chambers suggested we give power to certain things by dwelling on them. If we ignore them, then we strip away Satan's power.[5] Jesus reminds us in Matthew 16:23 that dwelling on our concerns shifts our thoughts away from God. He said, "Get behind me, Satan! You are a stumbling block to me; you do not have in mind the concerns of God, but merely human concerns" (NIV). God gives us all the tools we need to resist Satan. When we use them, we can tap into God's power and cause the devil to flee.

Dear God, help me to be on guard against Satan's temptations. Give me the power to resist.

Called to Create

He changes a desert into a pool of water and
makes water flow out of dry ground.
PSALM 107:35

The new homeowner pondered her large, empty backyard. She saw nothing but dirt and patches of dry grass. She didn't know exactly what she wanted, but she imagined her yard as a beautiful and peaceful retreat. She called in a landscape designer to help. Ideas rushed through the man's head as he surveyed the land. He sketched a plan that included trees, flower beds, a pond, and a fountain. His vision made what looked like a barren desert an oasis for the homeowner, a place where she could relax and find joy.

When God made us in His image, He designed us to be visionaries, to be creative with the skills and talents He gave us. Wherever God sees a blank canvas, He uses His imagination and wisdom to create a masterpiece. He calls us to do the same. Each day, He provides us with blank canvases begging to be filled. We build things, craft, sew, paint, cook, dance, make music. . . Whatever abilities God blesses us with, we can use them to bring joy and blessing to others. Think about how you can use your creativity today. Open your eyes to the blank canvases that await you. Then fill them.

Father, inspire me! Steer me toward using my skills and talents to bless others and serve You.

Motherhood

Bring up a child by teaching him the way he should go,
and when he is old he will not turn away from it.
PROVERBS 22:6

What an awesome responsibility to be a mother. God has already chosen all the women who will bring His children into the world and guide them to adulthood. God already knows the challenges each mom will face, the good days and the bad.

A quote often attributed to Mother Teresa says, "You will teach them to fly, but they will not fly your flight. You will teach them to dream, but they will not dream your dream. You will teach them to live, but they will not live your life. Nevertheless, in every flight, in every life, in every dream the print of the way you taught them will remain." Teaching children the way they should go does not guarantee they will follow your path. But Proverbs 22:6 provides hope that as children mature they will grow in wisdom and choose to follow Jesus' path to salvation.

God doesn't ask mothers to be perfect but only to do their best. A wise woman says to her son or daughter, "I will pray you through." The best thing she can do is surrender her children to God, pray for them, and entrust them to His care.

Lord God, please give me wisdom to parent my children. I put my trust in You to lead them and direct their steps from childhood through adulthood.

Quiet Waters

"Peace I leave with you. My peace I give to you.
I do not give peace to you as the world gives.
Do not let your hearts be troubled or afraid."

JOHN 14:27

"The Lord is my Shepherd. I will have everything I need. He lets me rest in fields of green grass. He leads me beside the quiet waters. He makes me strong again" (Psalm 23:1–3). These words have comforted people for generations. Trusting in God's love, goodness, and faithfulness can provide peace even when we feel troubled or afraid.

Horatio Spafford, author of the hymn "It Is Well with My Soul," found this to be true. He wrote:

When peace, like a river, attendeth my way,
When sorrows like sea billows roll;
Whatever my lot, Thou has taught me to say,
It is well, it is well, with my soul.

Spafford penned these lyrics while on his way to Wales to be with his wife, Anna. She and their four daughters had been on a ship that collided with another. The girls drowned. Anna survived.[6] Amid his heartbreak, Horatio Spafford clung to his faith and found a kind of peace that comes only from God: "And the peace of God, which transcends all understanding, will guard your hearts and your minds in Christ Jesus" (Philippians 4:7 NIV).

Heavenly Father, lead me to rest beside quiet waters. Send a gentle river of peace flowing into my soul.

I Will Never!

God has said, "I will never leave you or let you be alone."
HEBREWS 13:5

After celebrating the Passover meal together, Jesus and His disciples went out to the Mount of Olives. Jesus prepared them for what lay ahead. He said to them, "All of you will be ashamed of Me and leave Me tonight" (Mark 14:27). Peter replied, "Even if all men are ashamed of You and leave You, I never will" (verse 29). He said, "Even if I have to die with You, I will never say that I do not know You" (verse 31). The other disciples agreed. Then, just moments later, men came with swords and sticks, and they arrested Jesus. All the disciples left Him and ran away (verse 50). Even Peter, who vehemently said he would never leave Jesus, denied that he knew Him. Later, when Peter thought about that, he cried (verse 72).

As firm as we are in our faith, we still may find ourselves running from Jesus. We may be afraid of losing our jobs, friends, social positions, or even our lives by admitting we follow Him and everything He stands for. Just like Peter and the others, when our faith is tested, we sometimes run. Yet we must remember that even if we leave Jesus, He will never leave us. He understands our weakness, and He readily forgives.

Oh Jesus, I'm sorry. Forgive me for those times I've run from You or stayed quiet about my faith.

Eye of the Beholder

He has made everything beautiful in its time. He has put thoughts of the forever in man's mind, yet man cannot understand the work God has done from the beginning to the end.

ECCLESIASTES 3:11

Three friends stood gazing at the thick, textured white paint spread across a stark white canvas. "This doesn't belong in a gallery," said one. "I don't get it!" said the second. The third stood quietly pondering what the artist might have been thinking. "What a lovely landscape!" she said.

The phrase "Beauty is in the eye of the beholder" is used to express that people perceive things in different ways. The three friends are an example. The first saw what was negative, the second couldn't understand what she saw, and the third meditated on the piece of art and found its beauty. We can be quick to judge what we see and quick to dismiss what we don't understand. But when we ponder for a while and try to see through God's eyes, we discover He makes everything beautiful in its time.

There is plenty of ugly in the world and much that is difficult to understand. We can choose to dwell on the ugly and incomprehensible, or we can do our best to see through the eyes of God His beauty all around us. What will you see today?

Father, help me to find beauty amid what is ugly or beyond my understanding.

All You Need Is Love

God is love.
1 JOHN 4:8

In 1967, the iconic British band the Beatles recorded "All You Need Is Love." Like many of their songs, this one became a hit. It is a simple song with a simple message—love leads where you need to go; love provides confidence for what you need to do; love is all you need. While the song has nothing to do with Christianity or God, its message is biblical. The Bible says, "God is love" (1 John 4:8). "Love" leads us, gives us confidence, and supplies all our needs (Philippians 4:19). Love (God) is all we need.

Romans 8:38–39 tells us, "Nothing can keep us from the love of God. Death cannot! Life cannot! Angels cannot! Leaders cannot! Any other power cannot! Hard things now or in the future cannot! The world above or the world below cannot! Any other living thing cannot keep us away from the love of God which is ours through Christ Jesus our Lord." Notice these are not just statements. They are exclamations! *Nothing* can keep us away from God's love because God *is* love. When we accept Jesus (who is fully God) into our hearts, God's love is with us now and forever. All we need is love—His love. His perfect, infinite love.

Dear Father God, thank You for loving me today and for always!

"Mom, I'm Hungry!"

All Scripture is God-breathed and is useful for teaching, rebuking, correcting and training in righteousness, so that the servant of God may be thoroughly equipped for every good work.

2 TIMOTHY 3:16–17 NIV

Imagine you just got home from a long and stressful day at work when, minutes later, your husband arrives with your kids. Your teenage son gives you a quick hug and says, "Hi, Mom, what's for dinner?" You haven't prepared anything, but still, you are ready. You have all the ingredients you need for a quick meal that will satisfy his hunger.

God puts you in charge not only of satisfying your child's voracious appetite for food but also of feeding his or her emotional and spiritual hunger. Growing children have growing appetites for support and guidance. If you have stored God's Word in your heart, then you are ready to meet those needs. In Psalm 119 David says, "Your Word have I hid in my heart" (verse 11). Timothy says God's Word "is useful for teaching, rebuking, correcting and training in righteousness." If you read the Bible and meditate on its words, if you memorize scripture and store it inside your heart, then you will have all the ingredients ready for when your child is hungry for advice, comfort, support, or reassurance.

Make me ready, Lord God, to meet my child's every need by sharing and applying the wisdom of Your Word.

Strong Roots

Good will come to the man who trusts in the Lord, and whose hope is in the Lord. He will be like a tree planted by the water, that sends out its roots by the river. It will not be afraid when the heat comes but its leaves will be green. It will not be troubled in a dry year, or stop giving fruit.

JEREMIAH 17:7–8

When planting a tree, you need to dig a hole that is deep and wide enough for the roots to grow. You also need to gather information and follow instructions for proper planting and care. By applying what we learn, we can ensure that the tree grows healthy and strong with well-established roots.

Jeremiah 17:7–8 compares those who trust in the Lord to well-planted trees. Planted correctly and near a source of water, they form strong roots that will sustain them through times that are hot and dry.

Trusting in the Lord involves digging into the Bible to understand God's character, His ways, His promises, and His actions. Instead of just reading the Bible, we must immerse ourselves in it and absorb its teachings. It also means asking God for wisdom to apply His words to our lives. When we know and apply God's Word, then we will develop strong roots that nurture a healthy faith.

Lord, remind me to stop and think when I read my Bible so that its words will take root deep inside my heart.

The People We Meet

Do not forget to show hospitality. . .for by so doing some people have shown hospitality to angels without knowing it.

HEBREWS 13:2 NIV

A city dweller in the early 1900s, author Ray Stannard Baker imagined living in the countryside. Writing under the pseudonym David Grayson, Baker penned a series of books imagining the experiences he might have and the people he would meet while wandering country roads.[7] Farmers, beekeepers, a poet, a tramp. . .Grayson found something interesting in everyone he met, and he considered them new friends. In the introduction to his book *The Friendly Road*, he says, "It grows more wonderful every year how full the world is of friendly people! . . . We'll take toll of these spring days, we'll stop wherever evening overtakes us, we'll eat the food of hospitality—and make friends for life!"[8]

Each day, God sets new people on the paths we take. Some might be "human angels"—real people God sends to help us in some way. Some will stay with us for a while, and others will become lifelong friends. The world is filled with friendly people, God-loving people who can make our lives richer and fuller. Keep your eyes open for them. Add them to your circle of friends.

Father, remind me to be welcoming to the new people I meet. Guide me toward forming friendships with those who love and honor You.

. . . But What You Want

He said, "Father, if it can be done, take away what must happen to Me. Even so, not what I want, but what You want."
LUKE 22:42

Jesus knew what lay ahead. The plan was in place from the beginning. He would sacrifice Himself to save us from the punishment for our sins. Time had run out. It was about to happen. Luke 22:44 says Jesus was in agony as He prayed to ask His Father if there could be another way, and then Jesus surrendered the outcome to God: "Not what I want," He said, "but what You want."

Words have power. When we tell God, "Not my will, but Yours," we say we are willing to accept the outcome even if it's hurtful. It's like standing at the edge of a cliff in a windstorm, knowing that God will either calm the storm or allow you to fall. It's having confidence that if you fall He will catch you. "Not what I want, but what You want" is a bold prayer, a prayer built on faith that whatever happens, God will bring you through it. Are you willing to pray such a prayer? Would you still trust in God and have faith in Him if, like Jesus, you didn't get what you wanted?

Oh God, help me to have faith that even if a situation doesn't turn out the way I want, You will carry me through whatever lies ahead.

What Do You Think of Me?

"'For I know the plans I have for you,' says the Lord, 'plans for well-being and not for trouble, to give you a future and a hope.'"

JEREMIAH 29:11

Jeremiah 29:11 reminds us that God's plans for us are good. The King James Version has a slightly different translation. It begins, "For I know the thoughts that I think toward you." You might have asked God, "What are Your plans for me?" But have you ever asked Him, "What do You think of me?"

What do you think of yourself? Are your thoughts toward yourself gentle and nurturing, or are they deprecative and critical? God's thoughts toward you are always loving and gentle. You are His beloved daughter. He enjoys talking with you and hearing your voice. When you think you can't, God says you can. He says you are worthy. Any criticism God has, He offers gently, not to punish you but to help you reach your full potential. When you hurt, God wraps His strong arms around you and whispers sweet words of comfort and encouragement. He promises never to leave you. He lifts you up and never cuts you down. When you feel you aren't good enough, worthy of love, successful, important. . .shut out those belittling thoughts and ask Him, "God, what do *You* think of me?"

Loving Father, help me to think about myself the way You think of me.

Take Me on an Adventure

"Call to Me, and I will answer you. And I will show you great and wonderful things which you do not know."
JEREMIAH 33:3

"God, take me on an adventure." It's a bold prayer inviting God to accompany you on a journey to an unknown destination. Are you willing to pray such a prayer, or are you apprehensive?

Consider this: What if you asked your husband to take you on an adventure? If you trust him, you look forward to the ways he might surprise you and the new things you could see and do. His plan could test your skills or even lead to overcoming some of your fears, but you would trust your husband never to leave you or put you in danger. Sometimes we may find it easier to trust the people we love than to trust God.

Jesus said He came that we might have life—a great, full life (John 10:10). God has great and wonderful things to show us if we put our trust in Him. On any adventure, we expect the unexpected and some bumps along the way. But looking back, we see how our adventures led us to become better, stronger, and wiser. You were meant to live a life of adventure. Amazing things lie ahead if you just trust God to lead you.

Take me on an adventure, Lord.
Show me great and wonderful things.
Surprise me, challenge me, and teach me.

It Takes Two

Two people are better than one, because they get more done by working together.
ECCLESIASTES 4:9 NCV

Most do-it-yourself projects require a helper. When you and your husband worked together on a project, you probably heard (or said), "Honey, hand me that." "Honey, hold this." "Honey, grab that end, I'll take this end, and we'll carry it together." Working as a team got the job done, but at times it wasn't easy. The two of you disagreed. Your patience waned. You both got tired and irritated and maybe wanted to quit. But you hung in there. Later you looked back at what you had accomplished and saw that it was good.

Marriage is not a do-it-yourself project. It requires teamwork, patience, forgiveness, and endurance. Think of all the times you and your husband have solved problems together, carried burdens together, and supported each other. It wasn't always easy, but looking back you can see what you've accomplished. The two of you are better together. You have double the strength to face difficulties, and if either of you stumbles or falls or gets hurt, the other is there to help. Thank God that you have a partner to share life with and to help carry the load.

Thank You, Lord, for my husband. We've had some bumpy times in our marriage, but we survived. Thank You for helping us overcome the obstacles. Thank You for keeping us together and making us good together.

When You Worry

Do not worry yourself because of those who do wrong.
PROVERBS 24:19

Crime is everywhere—robberies, shootings, kidnappings, murders. Countries are at war. Every day we hear about civil unrest, terrorists, gangs, and drug cartels. People are divided over politics and ideas about what's right and what's wrong. Add to that the pandemic and wondering if it could happen again. We worry about our kids and grandkids having to navigate life in a world that is so chaotic and out of control. . . We worry about so many things.

When we worry, our faith atrophies. Worry is a key weapon in Satan's arsenal. He uses it to siphon our trust. Drained of faith, we become vulnerable to soak up all the world's troubles. Anxiety and fear creep in. We doubt. We wonder where God is and if He even exists—and Satan loves every minute of it.

Jesus tells us not to worry about tomorrow (Matthew 6:34). Paul reminds us not to worry but to pray (Philippians 4:6). In Ephesians 4:27, Paul warns us, "Do not let the devil start working in your life." So be careful. Be aware. Keep worry from stealing your peace and overriding your faith.

Dear God, I'm guilty of allowing worry to occupy my thoughts. Help me to remember You are bigger than all my worries. Give me faith beyond what I can see.

Seasons

There is a special time for everything. There is a time for everything that happens under heaven.

ECCLESIASTES 3:1

In her novel *Their Eyes Were Watching God*, author Zora Neale Hurston writes, "There are years that ask questions and years that answer."[9] This is true of the seasons of life.

Spring and summer are seasons filled with asking. In the spring of life, children ask questions because they want to fully understand what they are seeing and experiencing. Summer is a time of questioning life's messiness. Why didn't I get that job or promotion? Why did my boyfriend (or husband) leave me? Why can't I do more, try harder, and be better?

Fall ushers in a season of answers, of examining and reckoning lessons learned in spring and summer. It's when we measure, evaluate, and plan for winter.

Finally, winter brings wisdom and reconciliation. It's a time of settling in and looking back, hopefully without regret.

God created each season of life to mold and shape us to fit His plan. Whatever season you are in right now, do your best to live it with your eyes set on God. Live it fully and live it well.

Lord, shape me. Make me the woman You want me to be. Help me to live each season of my life with wisdom, gratitude, and joy.

Be Strong and Unafraid

But Moses said to the people, "Do not be afraid!
Be strong, and see how the Lord will save you today."
EXODUS 14:13

Moses led the Israelites out of slavery in Egypt. While camped on the shore of the Red Sea, they saw Pharoah and his army of soldiers on horseback and in war wagons coming for them. The people cried out to Moses, "'It would have been better for us to serve the Egyptians than to die here.' But Moses said to the people, 'Do not be afraid! Be strong, and see how the Lord will save you today. . . . The Lord will fight for you. All you have to do is keep still'" (Exodus 14:12–14). God said to Moses, "Lift up your special stick and put out your hand over the sea, and divide it. Then the people of Israel will go through the sea on dry land" (verse 16). So Moses did what God said, and the Israelites walked through on dry land to the other side. Then the walls of water closed over Pharoah and his soldiers, destroying them.

Whatever kind of trouble is chasing you today, know that God will fight for you. He will make a way for you to get through it. Be strong. Don't be afraid. Be still and see how the Lord will save you.

God, You know the trouble I face today.
Please come—fight for me and save me.

Memories

I thank God for you whenever I think of you.
PHILIPPIANS 1:3

Memories are a gift from God, another of His precious blessings. When we recall the good times we've spent with others, our memories make us smile. When distance separates us, reminiscing keeps loved ones near to us inside our hearts. Fond memories help us to grieve. They provide comfort when a loved one dies. Thoughts of good times we've shared help us hold on to a relationship even after a person is gone.

When Paul was in prison and separated from his friends, he wrote to them, "I thank God for you whenever I think of you." Paul's memories brought him peace and maybe even laughter and joy. He thanked God for the thoughts that sustained him.

A baby's giggle, a child's innocent question, the humorous misuse of a word, a friend's funny comment. A quiet caring conversation, a comforting hug, a gift of chicken soup when we're sick, a strong helping hand. . .we thank God for memories of those who love and care for us. Making memories bonds our relationships. Sharing memories extends God's blessings to others. It is a way of creating continuity that lasts decades.

What are some of your favorite memories? Share them with your children and grandchildren. Give them a glimpse of the history of *you*!

Heavenly Father, thank You for the happy times I've spent with family and friends. Thank You for the memories we've made together.

Changes

Jesus Christ is the same yesterday and today and forever.

Hebrews 13:8

Life is a revolving door of changes. Some we plan. Others surprise us. Whether you're a young woman with hopes and dreams, a mom juggling a job and family, an empty nester, or a retiree, life changes are ahead.

Change is inevitable. Navigating change is challenging and sometimes daunting. It requires adjusting to a new normal, settling in, or maybe even settling *within*. A breakup, a death, loss of a job, illness. . .some things in life force us to change and also to accept there are things we cannot change. Accepting can be hard, and for some people it can seem impossible.

One of the Bible's most comforting verses is Hebrews 13:8. It reminds us that when we get caught in a whirlwind of changes, Jesus is with us. He is just as strong, gentle, kind, powerful, and able as He was when He walked on earth. The character and power of Jesus do not change—ever! We can always count on Him to calm our fears, give us strength, and lead us through life's changes. He will guide us and help us look forward with faith and hope for the future.

What changes have you faced in the past five years? What brought you through them?

Dear Jesus, I trust You to guide me all the days of my life. Help me to meet every change with strength, faith, and hope.

What If?

He will not be afraid of bad news. His heart is strong because he trusts in the Lord.

PSALM 112:7

Roald Dahl often hid little gems of wisdom and life lessons in his children's books. For example, in *Charlie and the Great Glass Elevator,* he writes about "what-ifs" and how Columbus would have never discovered America had he let his uncertainties influence his actions.[10] In his book *The Twits,* Dahl talks about positive thinking and how a person who has a positive attitude "cannot ever be ugly." Good thoughts shine from the inside out.[11]

We teach our children not to worry and to have good thoughts, but as adults, we too are guilty of "what-iffing." Psalm 112:7 is a reminder to ward off every what-if that enters our minds. *What if I don't have enough?* Trust in the Lord! *What if I fail?* Trust in the Lord! *What if I get sick?* Trust in the Lord! If you trust in Him and get in the habit of replacing worrisome what-if thoughts with faith-filled thoughts, His love will shine through you like a sunbeam.

Lord God, fill my mind with thoughts of Your goodness. Let Your love shine through me for all to see.

'Round and 'Round

You can't whitewash your sins and get by with it;
you find mercy by admitting and leaving them.
Proverbs 28:13 MSG

A bad habit is like a merry-go-round. It goes 'round and 'round until the operator stops the ride. Maybe you've tried to eat healthier, exercise more, be on time, spend less time on social media. . . You might have become upset with yourself, struggled with guilt, given up, or even convinced yourself your bad habit isn't so bad after all.

Bad habits are another of Satan's subtle tricks. We do something once and do it again and again until the habit becomes as automatic as getting dressed in the morning. It's not until the Holy Spirit says, "This isn't good!" that we decide it's a habit we need to break.

To break a bad habit, recognize it comes from Satan, who is trying to lead you away from anything good. Confess your habit to God. Accept responsibility for it. Fight it! Trust what Paul says in 1 Corinthians 10:13: "God is faithful. He will not allow you to be tempted more than you can take. But when you are tempted, He will make a way for you to keep from falling into sin." Know that it will take time and that even if you fail, God will show you mercy and help you to try again.

Father, show me the way out. Help me to break this habit by focusing my thoughts on You.

Obedience

Observe the commands of the LORD your God, walking in obedience to him and revering him. For the LORD your God is bringing you into a good land—a land with brooks, streams, and deep springs gushing out into the valleys and hills.

DEUTERONOMY 8:6–7 NIV

When you tell your children to do something and they ask why, do you answer, "Because I said so"? You set rules because you want your children to learn respect. You want to lead them toward living good, godly lives. When they ask why they must obey, an explanation isn't always necessary. You expect obedience.

In Deuteronomy 8:6–7, Moses is speaking to the Israelites. After forty years of wandering in the desert, their journey is nearing the end. Moses reminds them of God's goodness, His blessings, and His power. They are about to enter the Promised Land, a beautiful land filled with brooks, streams, and springs flowing through hills and valleys. Moses reminds them to obey God's commands and honor Him because God desires all that is right and good for them.

We are God's children. No matter our age, God expects us to obey and honor Him even when we question His ways and commands. God has hope for us and good plans for our future when we obey Him and follow His rules.

Dear God, I know You want what's best for me, but sometimes, just like my children, I'm guilty of disobeying You. Please forgive me.

Peace at Any Price

"Blessed are the peacemakers, for they will be called children of God. Blessed are those who are persecuted because of righteousness, for theirs is the kingdom of heaven."

Matthew 5:9–10 NIV

Collins Dictionary defines the idiom "at any price" this way: "If you want something at any price, you are determined to get it, even if unpleasant things happen as a result."[12] Peace at any price usually has a negative connotation meaning that people are willing to do anything at all, even if it's evil, to get what they want.

The phrase has a positive meaning, though, when applied to what Jesus says in Matthew 5:9–10. As children of God, we are called to bring peace where there is division. We are called to act and speak as Jesus would to solve problems and bring people together. We're called to live out our faith even if we are disliked or persecuted for doing so.

Maybe you and your friends are divided over politics, or you don't see eye-to-eye on how to solve a problem. There might be division in your family, people not getting along or not speaking. Think about ways you can bring peace into those situations. Ask God to help you be understanding and forgiving. Trust that He will bless you even if others reject your attempts at peace.

Heavenly Father, help me to be a peacemaker. Give me the capacity to be understanding and to forgive when I'm persecuted for doing what's right.

Here I Am

Then I heard the voice of the Lord, saying,
"Whom should I send? Who will go for Us?"
Then I said, "Here am I. Send me!"
ISAIAH 6:8

Imagine you needed help. You called out your husband or child's name and asked, "Where are you?" You trusted them to answer, "Here I am," and to help with whatever you needed.

Similarly, God called out to Jacob, Samuel, and Isaiah because He needed their help. When He called to them, each man answered, "Here I am." God called them to do His work here on earth. God still calls on His people for help. What God asks us to do might seem insignificant, but we can't know the domino effect it will have in the grand scheme of things. When God called Jacob, He told him simply to return to Canaan, the land where he was born. Jacob obeyed. Later, Jacob became the founder of the great nation of Israel. Isaiah and Samuel were called to speak God's words to His people—prophecies about Jesus, the Messiah, which eventually led to His gift of salvation.

When we feel in our hearts God calling our names, we know He trusts us to carry out His will. When we answer, "Here I am, Lord," we can be certain He will lead us. Listen. Is He calling your name today?

Father God, I'm ready and willing to serve You. Here I am, Lord. How can I help?

No Thanks

"Be sure you do not do good things in front of others just to be seen by them."
MATTHEW 6:1

Christine's daughter said, "Mom, there's a new girl in school. I heard her family was homeless, but they just rented a house. Do you think we can help them somehow?" Christine and her daughter went through their closets and cabinets and put together a care package of clothing and food. They added a note and a gift card to a local grocery store. Mother and daughter went to the girl's house. The lights were on, and they heard the television inside, but no one answered the door. They left the package on the porch. As they drove away, they saw someone bring the gifts inside. In the days following, there was no response. Christine and her daughter felt disappointed and even irritated not to have received an acknowledgment and thanks.

Most of the time, we receive thanks for our good deeds, but when we don't get a thank-you, we need to remember why we give. In Matthew 6:1, Jesus warns us not to do good things so others will think well of us. He says to give expecting nothing in return (Luke 6:35). When we give, we give in Jesus' name. We give in service to Him.

Dear Jesus, help me to give in the way You give, with compassion and generosity, expecting nothing in return.

Comfort Them

He gives us comfort in all our troubles. Then we can comfort other people who have the same troubles. We give the same kind of comfort God gives us.

2 CORINTHIANS 1:4

If you ask doctors, nurses, and first responders why they chose their career, many will say it was because in their life they had faced some kind of trouble. Experiencing hardship, sadness, or pain made them more understanding toward those with similar problems. They chose their careers to provide help and comfort.

Paul said the comfort we receive when we're hurting teaches us to be more empathetic and caring. Paul had his share of troubles, but through them all he'd learned to stay focused on God. He found comfort through prayer, reflection on God's love and goodness, and his friends' kind words and acts.

God didn't promise us a pain-free life, but He did promise to accompany us through the pain. We find comfort in reading the Bible, talking with God in prayer, and interacting with those He sends to help us. Through our troubles we learn to comfort others with a loving hug, gentle, caring words, or just our quiet presence. We can't take away someone's trouble, but with empathy, we can assure them of God's love and help them walk through the pain.

Lord, You have brought me through my trouble; now help me to comfort others with kindness, compassion, and love.

Misunderstood

It is not the most important thing to me what you or any other people think of me. Even what I think of myself does not mean much.
1 CORINTHIANS 4:3

Paul and other early Jesus followers faced harsh criticism. Their mission to share the gospel was often misunderstood. They worked hard for no money and experienced hunger, thirst, and sometimes homelessness. People had little respect for them. Some thought they were crazy. Paul wrote in 1 Corinthians 4:13, "People think of us as dirt that is worth nothing and as the worst thing on earth to this day." He also said, "[Still] we speak kind words to those who speak against us. When people hurt us, we say nothing. When people say bad things about us, we answer with kind words" (verses 12–13). Paul didn't allow those who misunderstood to upset him. "It is not the most important thing to me what you or any other people think of me," he said. "Even what I think of myself does not mean much." Paul was Jesus' servant, and what mattered most was what Jesus thought of him.

Maybe you feel misunderstood or that your thoughts and opinions don't matter. Reframe your thinking to match Paul's. What's most important isn't what people think of you—or even what you think of yourself. Knowing your thoughts, actions, and words please the Lord is what matters.

Jesus, thank You for understanding me when others don't. I live to serve You.

He Loves Me!

I pray that you will be able to understand how wide and how long and how high and how deep His love is.

EPHESIANS 3:18

When you had your first boy crush, maybe you played this game. You asked, "Does he love me?" Then you plucked the petals off a flower, alternating between "He loves me" and "He loves me not." The last petal provided the answer. Of course, it was only a game. True love can't be determined by playing games or by trusting superstitions.

Do you wonder if God loves you? He loves you so much that He sacrificed His only Son so you could be made pure enough to live forever in heaven. Romans 8:38–39 says nothing will ever separate you from God's love. Ephesians 3:18 reminds you that His love for you is so big it's beyond your understanding. God's love for you is everlasting (Jeremiah 31:3). If you ever doubt His love, don't trust your feelings. If you ask, "Does He love me?" the answer is yes! Even when you've made a mess of your life, even when you need Him and He seems far away, God loves you. He loves you right now and He always will.

Thank You, Father, for the immense, unchanging, and tender ways You love me. Help me never to doubt Your love.

But Does He Like Me?

The Lord *delights in those who fear him,*
who put their hope in his unfailing love.
Psalm 147:11 NIV

You're having a bad day. You woke up grumpy and your attitude went downhill from there. You feel irritated and disagreeable. A few choice words have entered your mind, but thankfully they haven't escaped your lips. Earlier a coworker passed by and casually asked, "How are you doing?" "I'm good," you said. And then you added lying to the list of your bad thoughts and sinful behaviors. "Lord," you prayed, "I know You love me, but You can't possibly like me today."

God might not like your thoughts and behavior, but He still likes you. He likes you because you recognize your sin, because you care what He thinks of you, and because you want to do better. We all have bad days when our thoughts, words, and actions don't please God. None of us is perfect. There is always room for improvement. But God knows our hearts. He delights in us when we seek His forgiveness. He understands us. He likes us even when our behavior isn't very likable. Our heavenly Father is always ready to shower us with His never-ending love, mercy, and grace. He likes us just as we are.

Lord God, on days when I'm ashamed of my behavior and thoughts, thank You for forgiving me. Thank You for not only loving me but liking me too!

The Critics

"I have told you these things so My joy may be in you and your joy may be full."
JOHN 15:11

Ethan played quietly while his mom and her best friend sat in the living room drinking tea and sharing the latest gossip. "She really needs to lose weight," Ethan's mom said. "And she overdoes her makeup," her friend replied. The women went on criticizing a mutual friend from their church until Ethan interrupted: "You guys always say bad things about her. I think she's a really nice lady." The women looked at each other in silent shame. Our children, in their innocence, sometimes speak God's words.

There is no joy in criticism, either in giving it or in receiving it. Instead, we find joy when we look for the best in others and speak well of them. Ethan's mom and her friend continued their conversation but this time discussed how easy it is to fall into the trap of criticism. They shared a prayer asking God to forgive them. Then they decided to list all the good things they could think of about their friend. The more they thought about it, the longer their list became. The women found joy in focusing only on the good things, and their decision to stop criticizing their friend brought God joy too.

Heavenly Father, forgive me for having eyes that judge and lips that criticize. Help me to look for the good in others and to lift them up instead of cutting them down.

Freedom, God's Gift

"Come!" Let the one who is thirsty, come. Let the one who wants to drink of the water of life, drink it. It is a free gift.
REVELATION 22:17

"Freedom to choose." Those words remind us we have the freedom to decide, speak about, and act on our beliefs. The concept of free will began in the Garden of Eden. God didn't create us to be His slaves. Instead, He allows us to choose whether to obey Him. Adam and Eve, when presented with the choice of obeying God or disobeying, chose to disobey (Genesis 3). Sin entered the world that day and it grew. It continues to grow as people choose disobedience over following God's will.

Freedom is God's gift. He persistently invites us, "'Come!' Let the one who is thirsty, come. Let the one who *wants* to drink of the water of life, drink it. It is a free gift." It's an open-ended invitation and a choice. God in His mercy is always ready to forgive our sins and to offer us the refreshment of spiritual nourishment, renewal, and, through Christ Jesus, eternal life. Choosing to obey God leads to feelings of love, joy, and peace. Ask Him to help you make wise decisions that please Him.

Father, each day I face scores of decisions, some big, some small. I know I'm responsible for the choices I make. Direct me toward those that please You.

Music to My Ears

Shout for joy to God, all the earth!
PSALM 66:1 NIV

Many of the psalms are songs written by King David. Some tell readers the instruments used to play the songs and suggest a specific tune to which they are played. We can imagine David writing his songs, playing a harp or lyre, singing, and even dancing. Music was one of the king's special talents. He was a composer, musician, singer, and music director. He used his songs to praise the Lord.

Consider this quote by the nineteenth-century English poet Minnie Aumonier: "There is always music amongst the trees in the garden, but our hearts must be very quiet to hear it."[13] God places His music all around us. In the din of our everyday lives, we can miss hearing it. Wind rustling through dry leaves, a rushing stream, a gentle rain, crickets and katydids chirping in the night. A buzzing bumblebee, a singing wren, the rumble of distant thunder. . . The sounds of nature wrap around us like a soft blanket. They sing God's compositions and praise Him all day long. Perhaps these sounds inspired some of David's songs.

Listen now. What do you hear? The earth is praising God, but your heart must be quiet to hear it.

Oh God, quiet my heart. Open my ears to the music of nature, the sounds of the earth that worship and praise You.

Get Fit

Growing strong in body is all right but growing in God-like living is more important. It will not only help you in this life now but in the next life also.

1 TIMOTHY 4:8

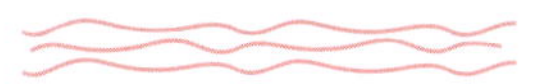

The fitness center is located at a corner with a stoplight that seems to stay red forever. Elaine often got the red light on her way to work. As she waited, Elaine watched women inside the center working out on treadmills and ellipticals and also lifting weights. She felt a wave of guilt. Some of her friends worked out. They had the bodies to prove it! Elaine knew it was good to get fit, but going to the gym wasn't her style. Had the apostle Paul sat in the passenger seat, he might have eased her guilt, saying, "Exercising your body is important, but becoming godly is more important. A spiritual workout is good for your soul."

A spiritual workout involves reading the Bible, meditating on its words, praying to God, and living in ways that please Him. The goal is to form a close bond with God and to become more like Him. As with any workout routine, it requires a daily commitment.

Do you have a fitness plan that includes strengthening your faith? If not, then make a plan and commit to staying with it.

Lord, I want a closer bond with You. Please guide me. Lead me toward having a stronger faith and a healthier body.

Learning to Listen

The purposes of a person's heart are deep waters,
but one who has insight draws them out.
PROVERBS 20:5 NIV

"I can't believe you're going to marry him!" Shannon said. "Yeah, well, I don't get why you don't like him!" Kate answered. Shannon and her sister, Kate, thought differently about many things, and that led to disagreements that ended in arguments. Had the women stopped talking *at* each other, listened well, and tried to be more understanding, the arguments might not have happened. Proverbs 20:5 is a reminder that some opinions run deep, but trying to get to the heart of why people feel as they do can lead to better understanding.

Insight begins with good listening skills. Jesus is the best role model. He listened with a caring heart, thoughtfully and without condemnation, and He refrained from interrupting or trying to redirect the conversation. He spoke in a quiet, gentle voice, asking purposeful questions in hopes of drawing out what was inside a person's heart. Jesus responded as a loving friend instead of someone with all the answers.

Becoming a good listener is a gift from God. It takes practice. It's another of those trying-to-become-more-like-Jesus things. Learning to listen as He did, to understand what's inside the heart, often leads to good results.

Dear God, help me to improve my listening skills. Teach me to listen as Jesus did, unrushed and intent on understanding. Let my responses be gentle and wise.

Let Your Light Shine

"Men do not light a lamp and put it under a basket. They put it on a table so it gives light to all in the house. Let your light shine in front of men. Then they will see the good things you do and will honor your Father Who is in heaven."

Matthew 5:15–16

Along with blessing us with special talents, such as singing, cooking, writing, and creating art, God also gives us people skills. These **social** skills help us work well and get along with others. Some of these social skills are patience, empathy, flexibility, a sense of humor, and the ability to resolve conflict. You likely can think of many more. Each of us is stronger in some of these skills than others.

Think about which people skills are your strongest. Now think about how you use them. God wants us to use our social skills to provide comfort and support. Friendliness and a sense of humor will brighten an otherwise dreary day. Patience will help someone succeed when they struggle to learn. The ability to reason and solve problems can unite people in harmony and understanding. Matthew 5:15–16 reminds us to use our skills to bring light into the world.

Make a conscious effort to use the skills you were blessed with. Let your light shine!

Lord, make me aware of my strongest people skills. Then teach me to use them to brighten the lives of others.

Rest for the Soul

Truly my soul finds rest in God; my salvation comes from him.
PSALM 62:1 NIV

In his book *The Pilgrim's Progress*, John Bunyan wrote about a pilgrim named Christian. Christian was ashamed of his sin. He carried its burden wherever he went until he came to the cross: "At the top of the hill stood a cross, and a little below at the bottom was a stone tomb. . . . Just as Christian came up to the cross his burden loosened from his shoulders and fell off his back. It tumbled and continued to do so down the hill until it came to the mouth of the tomb where it fell inside and was seen no more."[14] John Bunyan described what salvation feels like.

The forgiveness that comes with trusting Jesus as Lord and Savior frees us from the burden of sin. Imagine approaching the cross and confessing your sins to God. Then everything you've ever done that displeased God tumbles out of you and rolls into Christ's tomb where it vanishes, just as Christ's earthly body vanished.

Jesus says, "Follow My teachings and learn from Me. . . . You will have rest for your souls. For My way of carrying a load is easy and My load is not heavy" (Matthew 11:29–30). Our souls find rest in the miracle of salvation.

Dear Jesus, thank You for giving us the gift of salvation and for freeing us from the burden of sin.

When I Am Old

They will still bear fruit in old age, they will stay fresh and green, proclaiming, "The LORD is upright; he is my Rock."
PSALM 92:14–15 NIV

Maybe you've seen them, women aged fifty and older dressed in red hats and purple clothing. They belong to the Red Hat Society, a group for older women that stresses the importance of friendship, fun, and finding the good in life. The group describes itself as "reshap[ing] the view of women in today's culture."[15] You can't miss them in their red hats and purple clothes. They want to be seen to remind us that in our golden years we still have a purpose and a lot of living to do.

Older women have lived through many life experiences and are wiser and stronger as a result. They have wisdom to share with others. Anna in the Bible is a prime example. As an older woman with a close relationship with God, she possessed great wisdom. She was a prophetess who shared God's messages with the people. She bore fruit—doing God's work—well into her old age and stayed "fresh and green" by serving her Lord.

Even in old age when our bodies are tired and worn, God can still use us for His purposes. All we need to do is ask Him, "Lord, how can I serve You?"

Lord God, continue to use me when I am old.
Give me a purpose for the rest of my years.

Before I Speak

Even before I speak a word, O Lord, You know it all.

PSALM 139:4

"I knew I shouldn't have said anything," Angela told her husband. "I've only made things worse." Angela regretted the advice she'd given a coworker who was having problems with her boss. The coworker took Angela's advice, and now she was on probation. "I thought if she stood up for herself, he might have more respect for her," Angela continued. "But I was wrong."

Angela's intentions were good, but she hadn't thought about her words before she said them. Had she thought the situation through and prayed about it, Angela could have realized her advice might have negative consequences. She would have spoken with more wisdom or even said nothing at all.

The Bible says, "Wise people's minds tell them what to say, and that helps them be better teachers" (Proverbs 16:23 NCV). Wise people listen for God's voice inside their hearts. Angela had felt Him prompting her not to speak. She had a feeling she shouldn't tell her coworker what to do, but she ignored God's urging. Our Lord knows what we plan to say even before the words leave our lips. If we think our words might cause problems, it's important to wait before speaking and then ask God to guide us.

Heavenly Father, please give me a listening heart. Guard my mouth. Please remind me to consider my words before I speak.

Angry with God

As for me, I said, "O Lord, have loving-kindness for me. Heal my soul."
PSALM 41:4

In Shakespeare's play *The Taming of the Shrew*, Katherine says, "My tongue will tell the anger of my heart, or else my heart, concealing it, will break."[16] There is a little of Katherine in all of us—when deeply hurt, we release our pain through anger. When someone hurts us, we go to God and pray, "Oh Lord! What she did hurt me badly. Please take away my anger and heal my soul." But what if our anger is directed at God? What if we believe God could have prevented our hurt? Where do we go then? We go to God.

We need to know that it's okay to express our emotions to God, even when we're angry or hurt. Sometimes we experience pain as a result of someone else's poor choices or sin, and we may not understand why God allowed it to happen. But just like any loving parent, God wants to comfort us and help us through our pain. When we shut God out, we allow the devil to make our pain worse. However, when we trust God to help us, even when we're angry with Him, He will show us His loving-kindness, bless us with peace, and heal our souls.

Lord God, forgive me for being angry with You. Let me feel You near me. Comfort me and give me peace.

Our Ever-Present God

If I go up to the heavens, you are there;
if I make my bed in the depths, you are there.
PSALM 139:8 NIV

As Karla ended her sophomore year in college, she wasn't sure anymore that she wanted to be a teacher. She didn't know what she wanted to do, so she took a year off and joined an adventure club for young women. Always an outdoorsy girl and athletic, the idea of hiking, rock climbing, and exploring appealed to her. She challenged herself, pushed her limits, and climbed higher than she ever thought she could. The views were spectacular! Mountains draped in soft white clouds, sunsets melting into starlit skies. . . Karla explored caves and discovered underground chambers, rivers, and shimmering crystals. But most of all, in her travels Karla discovered God. His presence was all around her on earth, in the heavens, and underground. Karla returned to college, and today she teaches earth science in high school. In her spare time, she leads adventure groups and guides young women to Christ.

You don't have to travel to great heights or depths to find God. He is present in every quiet moment, in laughter shared with friends, in a song's melody, in the words of a book. . . Wherever you are, God is there. Where will you find Him today?

Oh God, I sense Your presence all around me.
It fills my heart with joy, peace, and love.

What a Friend!

The Lord spoke to Moses face to face,
as a man speaks to his friend.
EXODUS 33:11

What a friend we have in Jesus, all our sins and griefs to bear!
What a privilege to carry everything to God in prayer![17]

In 1855, Joseph M. Scriven's health was failing, and tragedy followed him like a dark cloud. His life was a mess. Neighbors disliked him for his eccentricities, he was broke, and he suffered from depression. Scriven understood hard times, and he helped others in their times of need. A poet by trade, Scriven wrote the lyrics to "What a Friend We Have in Jesus" to comfort his mother when she felt sad. Scriven understood we can talk with Jesus in prayer as one would talk with a friend. Jesus was, perhaps, Scriven's only true friend, and Scriven found comfort in talking with Him.[18]

Prayer is part of our personal relationship with Jesus. We don't need to speak our prayers with pious words as if we're quoting the King James Version of the Bible. Prayer is not speaking *to* Jesus. It is talking *with* Him. As long as we speak with honor and respect, we should talk with Him as we would a dear, intimate friend: candidly, honestly, and unguardedly.

Dear Jesus, when I confide in You, You provide me with whatever help and encouragement I need. You are always willing to listen and comfort me. Thank You, Jesus, for being my friend.

I Can't Go On

And let us run with perseverance the race marked out for us.

Hebrews 12:1 NIV

Nicole's sister, Abby, had end-stage cancer and was recently transferred to a hospice facility. Nicole had traveled the cancer journey with her sister for more than three years. They had no other living relatives, and the sisters were very close. Nicole did her best to meet Abby's needs while ignoring her own. She felt emotionally and physically spent and weary beyond words. She didn't know how she could keep going and face the tough days ahead. Nicole doubted she could persevere.

Sometimes the road we travel seems endless. Whether, like Nicole, we are caring for a critically ill loved one or working toward a seemingly impossible goal, we reach a point of weariness and wonder if we can go on. The Bible says we can. It holds many stories of people who thought they had reached their limits but persevered. Their strength came from God. "He gives strength to the weak. And He gives power to him who has little strength" (Isaiah 40:29). Nicole faced her sister's last days with strength as God walked her through each minute. Step by step, she persevered. Whatever trouble you face today, if you think you can't go on, trust God. He will give you strength.

Lord, I am so weary. There is no end in sight, and I don't think I can keep going. I need You. Give me the strength to persevere.

Before the Fall

If I must talk about myself, I will do it about the things that show how weak I am.
2 CORINTHIANS 11:30

The Bible tells of kings who lost everything because of their pride. King Uzziah did what was right in the eyes of the Lord. He prospered and accomplished great things. But power and fame led to pride, and pride resulted in Uzziah's downfall (2 Chronicles 26). The Bible includes several similar stories about prideful kings losing power and admiration when they didn't follow God: King Hezekiah, King Nebuchadnezzar, King Herod, the king of Tyre. . . Proverbs 16:18 says, "Pride comes before being destroyed and a proud spirit comes before a fall."

In 2 Corinthians, Paul reminds us to acknowledge our weaknesses (11:30). He says, "For when I am weak, then I am strong" (12:10). Admitting our faults to ourselves and others leads to humility. Some people are unable to recognize their flaws, which creates a false sense of superiority. Others are openly prideful, believing everything they do is above reproach. Isaiah 2:11 (NCV) says, "Proud people will be made humble, and they will bow low with shame." Acknowledging God's greatness, giving Him the glory for our accomplishments, and pursuing humility cause God's power working in us to increase our strength. When we put our faith in Him, and not ourselves, we prosper.

Oh Lord, guide me away from pride and lead me to humility.

Pride

Love does not remember the suffering that comes from being hurt by someone.
1 CORINTHIANS 13:5

Great film quotes, like "May the Force be with you," "There's no place like home," and "Love means never having to say you're sorry," stand the test of time. Quotes like these make us ponder and reflect on their meaning. For instance, is it really true that love means never having to say you're sorry? Maybe. But sometimes, even in loving relationships, our pride stops us from apologizing. We think to ourselves, *It wasn't that big of a deal, so why should I apologize?* Unfortunately, some people refuse to apologize even when they know they are wrong.

While love is patient, kind, and forgiving, pride is the opposite. Pride means never having to say you're sorry. It is selfish, stubborn, and foolish, and it can ruin relationships. Refusing to apologize sincerely can lead to weeks, months, years, even a lifetime of hurt and separation. As the character Count Dooku said in *Star Wars: Episode III—Revenge of the Sith*, "Twice the pride, double the fall."[19]

A genuine apology requires more than just saying, "I'm sorry." It also entails asking for forgiveness. Admitting one's mistake and saying, "Will you please forgive me?" means trading pride for humility. A genuine apology is offered with love and the hope of forgiveness, reconciliation, and restoration.

Heavenly Father, make me ready to admit my mistakes and apologize quickly, genuinely, and with sincere humility.

Simple Things

"Even little children and babies will honor Him."

MATTHEW 21:16

Adam and Katelyn considered whether to take their three-year-old son, Micha, on a camping trip to the lake. They worried he might be afraid of camping in an unfamiliar place. "We can always go home if it doesn't work out," Katelyn said. So they packed, assured Micha he would have a great time, and hit the road.

Micha helped Daddy set up the tent, feeling proud to be a "big boy." As they sat at the picnic table eating lunch, Micha shouted, "Look!" Several wild turkeys scurried off into the woods. "What are they? Can I pet them?" Micha continued asking questions about the world around him. "Why do fish live in water? Why does this place smell like Christmas? Why do campfires snap and crackle? How many stars are in the sky?" His parents patiently answered each one, explaining the wonders of God's creation.

As adults, we can become too busy to appreciate the simple things in this beautiful world created by God. But when we see His world through the eyes of a child, we can rediscover the joy and wonder. Take time today to notice the simple things in life—and then give honor and thanks to God for all the beauty that surrounds you.

Thank You, God, for revealing to me the beauty and wonder of the simplest things.

Two Lions

Be alert and of sober mind. Your enemy the devil prowls around like a roaring lion looking for someone to devour. Resist him, standing firm in the faith.

1 PETER 5:8–9 NIV

The lion, king of the beasts, is a symbol of power and strength. Its mighty roar can be heard for miles, making both humans and other animals fear and respect it.

The Bible compares the devil to a roaring lion looking for someone to devour. It warns us to be alert and sober-minded around the devil and to resist him by standing firm in our faith. We feel him lurking around us, waiting to attack. If we fear him, we increase his sense of power. As the nineteenth-century poet Samuel Taylor Coleridge observed, "Talk of the devil and his horns appear."[20]

The Bible's book of Revelation speaks of another lion, the Lion of Judah. This is a name given to Jesus Christ. When we put all our faith and trust in Jesus, He gives us the strength and power to resist the devil and he will flee (James 4:7). The devil fears Jesus' power. He knows that in the end, Jesus will return to earth and destroy him and all that is evil.

Two lions, one seeking to destroy us and the other wanting to save us. When we put our trust in Jesus, we have nothing to fear.

Lion of Judah, I place my faith in You and You alone.

Taste and See

Open your mouth and taste, open your eyes and see—how good God is.
PSALM 34:8 MSG

Emma and Camila met at a coffee shop to catch up on each other's lives. Camila ordered her usual hot black coffee. Emma ordered an iced vanilla latte with two pumps of raspberry syrup. "This is so awesome good!" Emma said. "Cold coffee?" Camila replied. "No way!" "Have you ever tried it?" asked Emma. "Yeesh. No, I wouldn't want to," said Camila. Had she tried just one sip, Camila might have discovered that she liked flavored iced coffee.

God's beautiful world holds so many things for us to try. Sadly, we sometimes prejudge whether we would like something before we try it. A quick judgment, imagining what something might taste or feel like, can keep us from new experiences we might enjoy. One person sees a photo of a charming little cottage tucked into the woods on the shore of a peaceful lake. She says, "I would love to live there!" Another looks at the same photo and says, "Imagine the mosquitoes! Living in the woods, I wouldn't feel safe." If we don't approach new things with a willingness to try, we might miss out on something wonderful God wants us to experience. Open your mouth and taste, open your eyes and see, how good God is.

Lord, remind me not to be so quick to prejudge new experiences. Give me the will and courage to try new things.

If I Knew Then

For if a man belongs to Christ, he is a new person.
The old life is gone. New life has begun.
2 CORINTHIANS 5:17

Little mistakes are forgotten. But big mistakes we remember with guilt, sadness, anger, shame. . .and we wish we hadn't made them.

Carol, a successful business executive, was unhappy with her career. Despite earning a generous salary, she felt miserable. Reflecting on her college years, she realized she had majored in business with the sole focus of making a lot of money. Carol's heart was leading her to teach, but she'd known on a teacher's salary she couldn't afford to buy her dream house, travel the world, or drive expensive cars. Now, as Carol looked back, she realized she'd made a big mistake that sent her in the wrong direction. She said to herself, "If only I'd known then what I know now."

If reviewing mistakes leads to sadness or self-loathing, be sure to ask God to turn your thinking around. Memorize Romans 12:2: "Let God change your life. First of all, let Him give you a new mind. Then you will know what God wants you to do. And the things you do will be good and pleasing and perfect." It's never too late to learn from your mistakes and to allow God to lead you to a happier life.

Father, please help me to let go of the past, and lead me toward a better future.

Just Say No!

Let your yes be YES. Let your no be NO. Anything more than this comes from the devil.
MATTHEW 5:37

"Mom, can you chaperone my class trip?" "Tracy, will you plan the spring luncheon for church?" "Mrs. Bell, you volunteered here at the food bank last year, and we could use your help again." Tracy Bell had a habit of saying yes to every request for help that came her way. She couldn't resist the urge to help others even if it left her feeling tired and with little time for her family and herself.

When Moses was doing too much, his father-in-law advised him to let others share the work. He said, "If you do this and God tells you to do it, then you will be able to keep your strength" (Exodus 18:22–23). It's okay to say no. God doesn't expect us to be superwomen. We should be willing to help. But when we say yes, it should be because we feel God leading us there. If we feel overextended and want to turn down an opportunity to volunteer, that can be God leading us too. Jesus said, "Let your yes be YES. Let your no be NO." Before you take on too much, ask God what He wants you to do. Then be sincere with your answer.

Dear God, if I'm unsure whether to say yes or no, I will rely on You to tell me.

Fulfilling His Purpose

For it is God who works in you to will and to act in order to fulfill his good purpose.
PHILIPPIANS 2:13 NIV

Have you ever had a time when everything you tried failed? When everything you touched broke, and every word you spoke caused trouble? Maybe you turned to music to soothe your soul, just as King Saul did. When Saul felt troubled, he said to his servants, "Find me a man who can play [the harp] well, and bring him to me" (1 Samuel 16:17). One servant said, "I have seen [David] a son of Jesse. . .who plays music well. He is a man with strength of heart. . .wise in his speaking. . . . And the Lord is with him" (verse 18). So Saul sent for David. Whenever Saul felt troubled, David played his harp, and then Saul felt better. Saul grew to love David. He said to Jesse, "Let David serve me, for he has found favor in my eyes" (verse 22). That one small act of the servant's recommendation was the first step on David's path to becoming Israel's greatest king.

God works in mysterious ways. When our lives intersect, it is not a coincidence. Only God knows how our interactions fit into His plan. Who knows? Today, some small thing you say or do might lead to something great.

Lord, please use me today to fulfill Your purpose, and may Your will be done through me.

Mad Cowper

I cried to the Lord in my trouble, and He answered me and put me in a good place.
PSALM 118:5

"God moves in a mysterious way, his wonders to perform; he plants his footsteps in the sea, and rides upon the storm. . . . Ye fearful saints fresh courage take, the clouds that you much dread, are big with mercy and will break in blessings on your head," wrote the eighteenth-century poet William Cowper.[21]

People called him "mad Cowper." Antisocial and reclusive, he spent his life in a state of hopeless depression. He attempted suicide multiple times, but each time he was unsuccessful. A Bible he found led Cowper to God and brought hope. A close friendship with John Newton provided someone who stood by him through all his troubles. But although Cowper knew the Lord and experienced waves of hope, he died feeling "unutterable despair."[22] God had tried again and again to save William Cowper. He saved him from suicide, tried to save him through His words in the Bible, and put Newton in his life, who also tried to save him. Still, despair seemed to surpass God's mercy in Cowper's life.

God wants to lift us out of trouble and put us in a good place. May we always set our thoughts on His mercy, His blessings, and His hope and never allow despair to ruin our lives.

Lord, let me be a vessel of hope to those facing depression. Help me to show them the light of Your love.

Lord, Teach Me

Lead me in Your truth and teach me. For You are the God Who saves me. I wait for You all day long.

Psalm 25:5

When she was twelve, Laurie accepted Jesus as her Savior. In the next several decades, she read the Bible, prayed, and went to church, but Laurie hadn't yet discovered the deep relationship one can have with the Lord. Although Jesus lived inside her heart, Laurie only thought of Him as living in heaven, and that put distance between them.

During a women's Bible study session, the leader began with a prayer: "Lord, teach us. . ." The women then discussed lessons they had learned from their personal relationships with Jesus. Laurie left the group that day wanting what they had: a closer connection with her Lord. She began praying differently. Each morning, she prayed, "Lord, teach me." She prayed, "Lord teach me," throughout the day, and at night she meditated on what she had learned. Soon, Laurie felt her relationship with Jesus becoming closer. She sensed the gap between heaven and earth lessen as Jesus worked inside her heart, teaching and leading her.

If your connection with Jesus feels somewhat distant, pray persistently for Him to teach you. Soon you will feel Him working in and through you, living within you, and guiding your path.

Lord, teach me. Teach me all day long and let me feel Your presence inside my heart.

Lost in a Crowd

From the ends of the earth I call to you, I call as my heart grows faint; lead me to the rock that is higher than I.
PSALM 61:2 NIV

Sonja was visiting her older sister, Nadia, who lived in a small town near New Delhi. Nadia had been teaching in India for several years, and unlike Sonja, she spoke Hindi fluently and was well-versed in the area's customs and culture. "I need to go to work for a few hours," Nadia told her sister. "It's best if you stay here. We'll do something when I get back." Sonja felt bored alone in her sister's apartment, so she decided to visit a nearby bazaar to buy some souvenirs. Eventually, the crowd became too big and overwhelming. Feeling anxious and afraid, Sonja realized she was lost and had left her cell phone at the apartment. "Lord, help me!" she prayed. Fortunately, she came across a kind couple who spoke English and, she discovered, were Christian missionaries. They helped her find her way back to her sister's apartment. Sonja was grateful and relieved to be back in a familiar place.

Wherever you are in the world, if you feel lost and need to find your way back home, you can call on God. He knows where you are, and He will lead you.

Lord, in this crowded, busy world, I sometimes feel lost and alone. Please guide me to where I will feel comfortable and safe.

Laugh a Little

He will yet make you laugh and call out with joy.

Job 8:21

Martin Luther King Jr. once said, "It is cheerful to God when you rejoice or laugh from the bottom of your heart."[23] Have you laughed today? Adding laughter to your daily routine can be a great way to brighten your mood. The first step is to learn not to take life too seriously. Think about what makes you laugh and make a promise to yourself to find something funny each day. You could try watching humorous videos, reading comics, or asking your children to tell you jokes. Allow yourself to be silly and do silly things, and you will surely find something to laugh about.

According to the Mayo Clinic, laughter is a great stress reliever. It stimulates the heart and lungs, increases endorphins, and can help relieve the physical symptoms of stress.[24] Laughter is like medicine for the soul. It enables us to take our focus off our troubles and the difficulties in the world around us. Cultivating a healthy sense of humor helps us get through the little bumps and irritations that disrupt our lives. Laughter is a gift from God, and He's pleased when our laughter is the result of good, clean fun. Who knows—maybe He even laughs with us!

Thank You, Lord God, for the gift of laughter. Please help me incorporate it into my everyday life.

Lord, Bless Me

And Jabez called on the God of Israel, saying,
Oh that thou wouldest bless me indeed.
1 CHRONICLES 4:10 KJV

Minor characters in the Bible can teach us valuable lessons, but they are often overlooked. Jabez is one of those characters. He is mentioned only in 1 Chronicles 4:9–10. His name means "one who causes pain." Jabez's mother gave him that name because of the pain she suffered in childbirth (1 Chronicles 4:9). Although we know very little about his life, we do know that Jabez prayed to "the God of Israel, saying, 'O, if only You would bring good to me and give me more land! If only Your hand might be with me, that You would keep me from being hurt!' And God gave him what he asked for" (1 Chronicles 4:10).

We can imagine Jabez worrying that his name's meaning was linked to his destiny. He prayed to God, asking for blessings and protection from harm. He also asked God to bring good to him and give him more land—greater authority and responsibility. From Jabez we learn to surrender our lives to God, ask for His blessings, and trust that He will provide what we need. Bring your requests to God today and ask Him to bless you.

Father God, bless me. Bless me abundantly.
Please protect me from evil that causes pain.
Bring good to me and guide me to do Your work.

Godly Mothers

Turn from sin, and do good.
PSALM 37:27

Every morning when she sent her son, Mason, off to school, his mother hugged him and said, "Do good." As Mason grew older, each time he left with his friends, she told him, "Do good." And when he got his driver's license, always before she handed Mason the car keys, his mother reminded him, "Do good."

The last time Mason could remember his mother saying those words was when she helped him move into his college dorm. As an adult, he faced many situations where he had to choose to do good or follow sin. Often he heard his mother's voice inside his heart saying, "Mason, do good." He felt her praying for him through job interviews, a cross-country move, troubles in his marriage, emotional hurt, and physical pain. Although he messed up sometimes, Mason tried to do good.

A godly mother's words resonate inside the hearts of her children. With Christ's love and guidance, she helps her children through challenges and prepares them for adulthood. Her prayers carry them through life. And when her children don't do good, a godly mother forgives them with grace and prays a little harder.

Dear God, teach me to represent the heart of Christ to my children. Help me to guide them into adulthood. And, Lord, I pray that whenever they face the temptation of sin, You will remind them, "Do good."

Stuck!

I waited patiently for the Lord. He turned to me and heard my cry. He lifted me out of the pit of destruction, out of the sticky mud. He stood me on a rock and made my feet steady.

Psalm 40:1–2 NCV

Life seems redundant sometimes. As in the movie *Groundhog Day*, the same day can seem to be repeated over and over until we cry out, "Help! I'm stuck! Get me out of here!"

Feeling stuck can be frustrating, especially when you feel trapped in your job or daily routine and don't know how to break free. The truth is you are not stuck. There is a way out, and you can find it today. First, pray. Ask God to lift your feet out of the sticky mud and set you on solid ground. Next, remember God gives you freedom to choose. You can either stay where you are or take a new path. Create a list of things you'd like to do if you weren't feeling stuck. Rank them by importance. Pray again and ask God to guide you. Then, start working toward one of your goals. Be patient. Surrender control to God and allow Him to lead you. When you stop focusing on your current circumstances and start expecting good things to happen, your path will be filled with possibilities.

Heavenly Father, I'm in a rut and I want to get out. Please lift me up and help me to move forward.

A New Song

He put a new song in my mouth, a song of praise to our God.
PSALM 40:3 NCV

The phrase "Sounds like a broken record" has its origins in the era of vinyl records. Back then, if you played your favorite song over and over, the vinyl could become scratched or worn, resulting in the song skipping and repeating the same part again and again. This was a sign that it was time to replace the record or move on to a new song.

Similarly, we find comfort in the familiar song of our lives, our routines and sights and sounds and the rhythm they create. But if we listen to our hearts, we may hear God calling us to a new song. He may be urging us to step out of our comfort zone and embrace a fresh opportunity.

Be brave and open to change. Trust that God has something new and exciting in store for you. Instead of clinging to the old, sing to the beat of a new song. Take ownership of the opportunities God presents to you, and He will guide you toward new paths of growth, satisfaction, and meaning. And when He blesses you with new opportunities, don't forget to express your gratitude and praise Him.

Lord, lead me to embrace new opportunities with joy and expectation. Help me to be brave and open to change.

Choices: A Blessing or a Curse?

The way of fools seems right to them, but the wise listen to advice.
PROVERBS 12:15 NIV

At the ice cream shop, Simone read the flavor list to her five-year-old daughter Rita. "The flavor of the week is Chili Chocolate" she said. Rita liked both chili and chocolate, so what could go wrong with combining those two? "I want that one," she said. "Are you sure?" her mother asked. "It might be spicy hot." Rita didn't believe that something cold could be hot at the same time. "Yes, I want that one," she confirmed. With her first taste, the little girl's eyes widened. She started frantically fanning her mouth. "It's hot!" she cried.

The choices we make can be a blessing or a curse. A quick decision before thinking through the consequences can lead to trouble, but decisions carefully considered can turn into a blessing. Proverbs 12:15 reminds us to seek wise advice. When we're faced with an uncertain decision, asking for advice is always a good choice. When we consider wise counsel along with listening for God's voice inside our hearts, making decisions becomes easier.

Are you facing an uncertain choice today? Ask a trusted friend for advice. Seek counsel from God's Word. Pray. Let God lead you.

Father God, sometimes I'm guilty of making quick decisions that don't turn out well. Please remind me to think before I act and to seek advice from family members and friends.

Your Greatest Asset

I know, my God, that you test the heart
and are pleased with integrity.
1 CHRONICLES 29:17 NIV

What is your greatest asset? Were your first thoughts about your body? Maybe you have beautiful skin, great legs, a sunny smile, perfect hair. . . But let's think instead about your heart. What personality trait would you consider your greatest? There are many great qualities to consider: patience, kindness, humility, forgiveness, generosity, persistence, compassion. . . But maybe the best of all assets is integrity—being honest and having moral principles that are pleasing to God. Without integrity, we lose credibility, honor, and trust. Instead of drawing people to us (and, by our example, leading them nearer to Christ), we send them running away, or worse, we lead them into a life of immorality and dishonesty.

Integrity at the foundation of our character helps us become more reliable, respectable, confident, and purposeful. It makes us accountable for our actions and helps us to live the kind of life Jesus lived. With integrity, we know we are inside God's will.

First Chronicles 29:17 is a scripture verse to memorize. Keep it close to your heart. When integrity is your greatest asset, you know you are pleasing God.

Lord, I want integrity as the foundation of my character. I want to please You with my honesty and willingness to live a good and moral life.

Putting Down Roots

Have your roots planted deep in Christ. Grow in Him. Get your strength from Him. Let Him make you strong in the faith as you have been taught. Your life should be full of thanks to Him.

COLOSSIANS 2:7

The 1977 miniseries *Roots* recounts the story of Kunta Kinte, a seventeen-year-old boy who was captured from his home in Gambia and sold into slavery in America. The show depicts the struggles, resilience, and quest for freedom of seven generations of his family, culminating in their eventual emancipation. It emphasizes the unbreakable bond of family and the connection that helps them survive and thrive.

While it is important to be rooted in our heritage to better understand ourselves, it is even more crucial to be firmly grounded in Christ. Jesus is the core of a family's growth and strength. If our roots are grafted to His, our family grows stronger. We can do little without Him, but with His help, we can flourish. A family whose foundation is rooted in Jesus will have the strength to weather any challenges that come its way. So ask Jesus to graft His roots to your family and to help it grow in love, faith, and commitment to Him.

Dear Jesus, I want my family to be wholly dependent on You. Please provide us with a firm foundation and help us to grow in our love for You and each other. Strengthen our faith and lead us to thrive.

Believe!

The angel said to her, "The Holy Spirit will come on you. The power of the Most High will cover you. The holy Child you give birth to will be called the Son of God."

LUKE 1:35

The story of the virgin Mary is one of the most amazing stories in the Bible. Imagine going about your daily routine when suddenly an angel appears and tells you that God has chosen you to give birth to His Son. Mary, confused and unsure, asks how this could happen, and the angel responds by saying that the Holy Spirit will come upon her and the power of the Most High will cover her. Mary, with her strong faith, believed the unbelievable, and God did exactly what the angel said. The Holy Spirit came to Mary, and she stepped into her role as the one chosen to bring Jesus into the world.

The story of Mary shows us that all things are possible with God. Even today, we hear of modern-day miracles: A tumor disappears without intervention, someone in a financial crisis receives an unexpected check for the exact amount they need, a woman whose doctors said she couldn't bear children miraculously becomes pregnant. . . God sends His Holy Spirit to us today just as He did to Mary. He wants us to believe for and expect a miracle, because with Him all things are possible.

God, by faith I believe that with You anything is possible. Help me to believe even more.

Work On Your Game

You servants who are owned by someone must obey your owners. Work for them as hard as you can. Work for them the same as if you were working for Christ.

EPHESIANS 6:5

Many Christian athletes pray for strength before games and give glory to God for their victories. This includes athletes in all sports—basketball, volleyball, gymnastics, baseball, football. . . Gabby Douglas, the first African American Olympic gymnast to win gold in the Women's Gymnastics All-Around, said, "I give all the glory to God. It's kind of a win-win situation. The glory goes up to Him and the blessings fall down on me."[25]

The Bible encourages us to work hard for those in positions of authority—indeed, to work as hard as we can in everything we do, as if we are working for the Lord. When we keep this instruction in mind, we can give our best effort even when dealing with tough coaches, difficult bosses, or demanding teachers. When we encounter challenging situations, we can pray and ask God to guide us toward a positive outcome. Whether we win or lose, we should remember to give Him the glory for giving us strength to persevere. When the glory goes up to Him, the blessings fall down on us.

Father God, whatever work I do, I want to work hard as if I'm working for You. Whether I succeed or fail, I will give You the glory for helping me to persevere.

Be Inspired

Above all, you must understand that no prophecy of Scripture came about by the prophet's own interpretation of things. For prophecy never had its origin in the human will, but prophets, though human, spoke from God as they were carried along by the Holy Spirit.

2 PETER 1:20–21 NIV

The Bible is the true and inspired Word of God. Although it was written by men, the words came from God Himself. The Holy Spirit worked through men to communicate the exact words God wanted them to write. Second Peter 1:20–21 reinforces the fact that the Bible's prophecies were given by God, while 2 Timothy 3:16 confirms that *all* scripture was inspired by Him.

The Bible inspires us to continue learning, to acknowledge and correct our shortcomings, and to lead a righteous life. Its words provide comfort and empower us. Its stories offer examples of those who obeyed God's commands and overcame challenges.

How have you experienced the impact of God's Word in your life? Maybe it has given you courage to try something new, strength to overcome a challenge, or solace in a time of sadness or loss. Make reading the Bible a part of your daily routine. Meditate on it, and allow its words to inspire you.

I am grateful, Father, for the gift of the Bible. May Your Holy Spirit continue to inspire me through its pages and guide me on the path of righteousness.

Be Gentle

Be gentle and kind. Do not be hard on others.
Let love keep you from doing that.
EPHESIANS 4:2

In Matthew 11:29, Jesus says, "I am gentle and do not have pride." Jesus is our role model for gentleness. Throughout the New Testament, we see many instances where Jesus treated others gently and with loving-kindness. Rather than be hard on people for their faults, Jesus responded quietly, carefully, and wisely. He told His followers, "I am sending you out like sheep with wolves all around you. Be wise like snakes and gentle like doves" (Matthew 10:16).

Acquiring the characteristic of gentleness can help us to become more loving and kind, not only toward others but also toward ourselves. Sometimes we can be extra hard on ourselves. It's good to recognize our faults and work on improving them, but dwelling on them can lead to anger and self-loathing. We need to be kind and gentle to ourselves, remembering that we aren't perfect and don't always act wisely. The Lord expects us to make mistakes. With gentle kindness He forgives us, loves us, and helps us to do better. He also wants us to forgive ourselves and to surrender any self-loathing to Him. So go easy on yourself, relax, and listen to Jesus' gentle voice speaking inside your heart. Allow Him to restore your soul.

Lord, help me to be kinder, gentler,
and more forgiving to myself and to others.

It's Good That I Love You

Most of all, have a true love for each other. Love covers many sins.

1 PETER 4:8

Newlyweds Ramon and Claire were adjusting to married life when they discovered annoying little habits about each other that irritated them. Ramon always left the cap off the toothpaste, and Claire was so well organized that Ramon found it difficult to find things. One day, Claire said, "It's a good thing I love you, or I'd be irritated." This lighthearted remark became a running joke between them, softening instances when they were annoyed with each other over little things. Over the years, this phrase strengthened their marriage and taught them not to get upset over little things.

The Bible teaches us that love covers many sins. It covers many habits too. True love doesn't let small issues grow into bigger problems. Love grows even stronger through forgiveness and understanding. Just as your husband may have habits that irritate you, you probably have some that bother him too. These irritations may change over the course of your marriage. If you can learn to accept these annoyances with love and even a bit of humor, your feelings of frustration just may fade away.

Father, I find myself getting annoyed over little things at times, not just with my husband but also with my children, coworkers, and others. Please help me to accept these little irritations with love and to remember that I'm not perfect either.

Decompress, Relax, and Unwind

When I was upset and beside myself,
you calmed me down and cheered me up.
Psalm 94:19 MSG

Jenny often wished she had the same athletic ability as her friend Shannon. Whenever Shannon felt upset, she would go for a long run. Shannon told Jenny that praying while running helped her to calm down and find peace.

If you're not into athletic activities like Jenny, there are still plenty of other ways to relax and decompress. The key is to find something you're passionate about. Engaging in a favorite hobby or activity while having a conversation with God can help take your mind off your troubles. Whether it's music, art, sewing, gardening, photography, or baking, the possibilities are endless. Read a cozy mystery, work a jigsaw puzzle, play a game, write poetry. . . Reduce stress by changing your environment. Visit a museum, an outdoor market, or a festival. Take a leisurely walk in the woods or by the water. Thank God for any sights and sounds that bring you joy. Lastly, pray and ask God to guide you. What healthy activity can the two of you do together today that will bring you peace and joy? Find your passion, whatever makes you happy, and work it into your daily routine.

Dear God, what is something fun we can do together whenever I feel stressed? Teach me to decompress, relax, and enjoy spending time with You.

We're in This Together

"I give you a new Law. You are to love each other. You must love each other as I have loved you."
JOHN 13:34

"God, why me? Yesterday the washing machine broke just as all my underwear was in the wash cycle. Today I got a flat tire on the way to my son's high school track meet, and now I feel like I'm getting a cold. Some days everything seems to go wrong. But I know I'm not alone, Lord. Everyone has their 'why me?' days."

On those days when a dark cloud follows us around, we need to remember that everyone is going through something. We are not alone. We're all doing life together. In John 13:34, Jesus commands us to love and support one another. Loving one another means being thankful for those who come to our aid. It means thinking about the troubles others face, praying for them, and helping them if we can. On those tough days, we can shift our focus to the love and help around us. Reminding ourselves that we're not alone and that we'll get through our troubles with God's help, along with the love and support of others, can make a challenging day a little easier.

Jesus, I'm having the kind of day when everything is going wrong. Instead of asking, "Why me?" I ask You to help me be hopeful. This trouble is temporary, and we'll get through it together.

God's Never-Ending Love

Now a river flowed out of Eden to water the garden. And from there it divided and became four rivers.

GENESIS 2:10

God created a river to water the Garden of Eden, which then divided and became four rivers. We can imagine this river as a metaphor for God's love. His love is a steady river constantly nourishing our hearts, enriching our souls, and strengthening our faith. Eventually the river divides into multiple streams, symbolizing God's love flowing through us to quench the spiritual thirst of others.

When we accept Jesus as our Savior, our hearts swell with God's love. His love is an eternal source of comfort, wisdom, strength, and perseverance, fulfilling all our needs. Psalm 1:2–3 says when we love His teachings and think about them day and night, we become strong like a tree planted by a river, a tree that bears fruit and has leaves that never die. When we seek God's river of living water, it is given to us freely. All we need to do is ask.

Allow the boundless love of God to fill your heart today, and then share it generously with others. Each time you share His love, you create a stream of hope, an invitation for others to drink from His river of living water, the river that never ends.

Heavenly Father, let Your love flow through me and spill over to nourish the hearts of others.

Who Are Your Allies?

In time of trouble, trusting in a man who is not faithful is like a bad tooth or a foot out of joint.
PROVERBS 25:19

Have you ever experienced the pain of being betrayed by a friend? Betrayal can be incredibly painful. You place your trust in someone only for them to break it. The emotional pain can be worse than a bad tooth or a broken foot, but it's a lesson learned—don't put your trust in someone who isn't faithful, not only to you but also to God.

A friend who loves the Lord is unlikely to betray you. Those who are committed to Him strive to do what is right. In your circle of friends be sure you have some strong allies, friends who share your faith and whom you know you can trust all the time. Friends like these are ones you can confide in, pray with, and ask for wise advice. Faithful friends will stand by you through both tough and joyous times, supporting you, laughing with you, crying with you, and praying for you.

To have allies, you also must be an ally. This means sharing your friend's struggles, celebrating her victories, and placing God at the center of your friendship. Healthy and enduring friendships are built on a foundation of trust and love. Who are your allies?

Lord God, please lead me to trustworthy friends. And guide me to be a faithful friend in return.

Run to Daddy

I run for dear life to God, I'll never live to regret it.
Psalm 71:1 msg

After you've been away from your children for a while, when you arrive home they run to you shouting, "Mommy! Mommy!" They wrap their arms around you and give you huge bear hugs. What a wonderful feeling it is when your children run to you joyfully, happy to be in your presence. You are their rock, their safe place. They run to you for love, and sometimes for comfort and protection.

When you pray, do you ever run joyfully to your heavenly Father? Usually we come to Him feeling guilty and seeking forgiveness or because there is something we want or need. We come quietly, respectfully, and with thanksgiving. All of that is fine, but how often do we run to the Father, just wanting to wrap our arms around Him and know that we are safe and loved? That's the kind of relationship He wants with us, where we run to Him shouting, "Daddy! Daddy!" as we trust in the safety of His embrace and joyfully bask in His presence. Close your eyes and imagine yourself running to your heavenly Father. He will welcome you with open arms.

Here I am, Lord. Here I am running to You, wanting and needing to be in Your presence. I run joyfully into Your welcoming embrace where I always feel safe and loved.

The Fast Lane

So be careful how you live. Live as men who are wise and not foolish.

EPHESIANS 5:15

Maryann was always in a rush. Wherever she went, she brought with her a flurry of activity and sometimes chaos. On the expressway on her way to work, Maryann drove in the fast lane, dodging in and out of traffic, passing slower cars in her way. As she approached her exit, she tried to get into the slower lane, but heavy traffic stopped her. Anger welled within her as she sailed past her exit. But then a quiet yet strong voice in her heart rose above the anger and said, "Maryann, slow down!"

Satan loves chaos. He loves when we live life in the fast lane, so rushed and consumed by our own desires that we forget about God. Living apart from God leads us to make foolish decisions. He wants us to slow down and be careful how we live. Maryann was blessed that day—blessed to hear God's voice and blessed to have merely missed her exit instead of causing an accident by the foolish way she drove.

In Ecclesiastes 2:13 (NCV) Solomon says, "Being wise is certainly better than being foolish, just as light is better than darkness." Let's be wise and get out of the fast lane. Let's listen to God and slow down.

Father, slow me down. Steer me away from life's chaos and fill my heart with Your peace.

We've Got This!

For we work together with God.
1 CORINTHIANS 3:9

The Scripps National Spelling Bee challenges participants to be the best at spelling difficult words like *koinonia*, *marocain*, and *gesellschaft*.[26] It takes winning a regional competition and a great deal of study to be accepted as a contestant. When spelling such difficult words, it helps to know the word's definition, part of speech, and language of origin.

Fourteen-year-old Aniya was entering the competition for her second year. Her goal was to win and nothing less. She pushed hard, studied relentlessly, and sometimes became frustrated to the point of tears when she couldn't remember how to spell a word. Aniya's brother and mother were faithful study partners. They always reminded her, "Don't worry. We've got this, God's got this, and we'll leave the rest to Him."

When we face challenges, God says to us, "We've got this!" He will partner with us in all areas of life. Our goals might not always align with His will, but win or lose, He promises that "all things will work together for the good of those who love Him and are chosen to be a part of His plan" (Romans 8:28). Ask your heavenly Father to align your plans with His will. Then partner with Him to work His plan together.

Father God, please be my partner. Guide me to align my plans with Your will and help me to accept the outcome, no matter what.

Nurture God's Word

"Some seed fell between rocks. As soon as it started to grow, it dried up because it had no water."
LUKE 8:6

Jesus said the Word of God is like seed. If planted well inside our hearts, it grows and produces good fruit. He said that some people receive God's Word with joy, but they don't allow it to take root. It is like seed that falls between rocks. As soon as it starts to grow, it dries up because it has no water. These people believe in the Word for a while, but Satan doesn't want them to believe, so when he tempts them, they give in and give up.

God's Word, the Bible, isn't meant only to be read. We need to ponder what we read, pray about it, ask God to enlighten us, and then apply His teaching to our lives. Believing what we read with faith, assured of its truth, is like watering the seed. It allows God's Word to take root in our hearts, to grow, and to produce fruit like wisdom, courage, and strength. When you read the Bible, go slowly. Think about its words. Let them settle into your heart and read them again and again. Make reading the Bible a priority, and never give in when Satan encourages you to stop.

Dear Lord, I will do my best to actively study Your Word and keep it well-watered inside my heart.

Your True Self

For there is nothing covered up that will not be seen.
There is nothing hidden that will not be known.
LUKE 12:2

The idiom "I can see right through you" means "You can't fool me. I know what you're really thinking." Someone's persona can be different from their true character. Their persona at work might be radically different from the way they act at home. The image they project at church can be the opposite of their character in certain social situations. The truth is that those who know us well can see beyond our masks. Even if we don't know our own true selves, they do. They can see right through us to the depths of our character.

Masking our true character can crush us with anxiety. It can lead to low self-esteem and leave us asking, "Who am I really?" Luke 12:2 says there is nothing covered that won't be seen, nothing hidden that won't be known. God knows our hearts. He wants our true selves to be a reflection of Him. When we focus on becoming more like Him, God will help us overcome our insecurities so His light will shine through us. Ask Him today to help you remove any masks and show the world the woman He made you to be.

Heavenly Father, I want to be real with others. I want my true self to reflect Your love. Let Your light shine through me for others to see.

Attitude Is a Choice

A glad heart is good medicine,
but a broken spirit dries up the bones.
PROVERBS 17:22

Eight-year-old Sophia hummed a happy song as she walked down the stairs. Skipping to the breakfast table, she chirped, "*Good* morning!" overemphasizing the word "good." "My, you're in a happy mood," said her mother. "I'm choosing to be happy," Sophia answered. "I don't want to go to school today, so I'm thinking about good things. It helps put me in a good mood." Sophia's Sunday School class had been studying Paul's words in Philippians 4:8 about keeping our minds set on everything good and worth giving thanks for. When Sophia put the Bible's words into action, she discovered that attitude is a choice.

As humans, we have the ability to change our attitude. By praying, meditating on God's Word, and putting it into action, we can exchange anger for forgiveness, laziness for willingness, apathy for empathy, and even hate for love. Dwelling on our blessings and God's love for us is like medicine. It resurrects a dying spirit and warms a cold heart. A good attitude doesn't necessarily mean we are overly optimistic. It means we are accepting of where we are right now, allowing Christ's peace to enter our hearts, assured He will see us through. Put on a good attitude today, and let your heart be glad.

Lord, as I set my thoughts on You and Your blessings, give me an attitude that's right and good.

In Weakness, I Am Strong

Out of the mouth of children and babies,
You have built up strength because of those who
hate You, and to quiet those who fight against You.
PSALM 8:2

Nothing is more precious than an innocent child's prayer. With humility and a sense of familiarity, she kneels down at her bedside and talks with her heavenly Father. God loves His little children. Even though they appear weak, He makes them strong. If you need proof, visit a hospital where children endure life-threatening illness with steadfast strength. God is the one giving them power to fight and providing "human angels" to comfort and care for them.

When we are weak, God makes us strong. He hears our prayers every time we cry out to Him for help. Even when we're adults, He sees us as His children, and we can be sure our Father will provide us with strength to endure whatever trouble comes our way. With each problem we overcome, God will build our faith and trust in Him. He makes us even stronger and ready to fight the powers that war against us. He promises, "My grace is sufficient for you, for my power is made perfect in weakness" (2 Corinthians 12:9 NIV). You can stand on that promise today and every day.

Father God, when I am weak, give me the strength to endure and fight. Give me the faith of a child, and help me believe that Your mighty power working within me will overcome any challenge I face.

God's Grace

And the God of all grace, who called you to his eternal glory in Christ, after you have suffered a little while, will himself restore you and make you strong, firm and steadfast.

1 PETER 5:10 NIV

God blesses us in many unique and wonderful ways. He loves us unconditionally, forgives our sins, and extends us grace, His undeserved favor.

When sin entered the world, it brought with it suffering. We suffer because of the actions of others, our own poor decisions, and Satan's evil power. But in our suffering, we can be assured of one thing: God's grace will restore us and make us strong, firm, and steadfast. His grace never ends, and He gives it to us freely.

We grow stronger in grace as we humble ourselves and come to a fuller understanding of God's unconditional love and forgiveness. Then, with God working through us, we can—and should—extend grace to others. God treats us better than we deserve, and He calls us to do the same: to be kind, forgiving, compassionate, and caring toward those who don't deserve it. Showing grace doesn't always come easily, but extending grace freely is one of the most important lessons we can learn.

Dear heavenly Father, thank You for Your unconditional, never-ending grace. Teach me to be an extension of Your grace by being kind, forgiving, and compassionate to everyone, especially the undeserving.

Dust in the Wind

All go to the same place. All came from the dust and all return to the dust.
ECCLESIASTES 3:20

It is impossible to think of the classic rock band Kansas without remembering their hit song "Dust in the Wind."[27] Its lyrics reflect some of the thoughts expressed by the author of Ecclesiastes, who says that striving to find lasting joy in worldly things is meaningless. "Dust in the Wind" suggests that our dreams, our possessions, and everything we do will eventually end and turn to dust. That's a sad and depressing thought, but for some it rings true. All the worldly things that bring them joy will end, and their lives will come to a close with nothing left but dust.

The author of Ecclesiastes ponders life further, more deeply, and from a different perspective. He concludes that life is meaningless without God. To the reader he says, "Remember. . .your Maker while you are young, before the days of trouble come and the years when you will say, 'I have no joy in them.' . . . Honor God and obey His Laws. This is all that every person must do" (Ecclesiastes 12:1, 13). Our earthly bodies will go to the same place and become dust, but by God's gracious redemption of us through Jesus, our souls will receive new, heavenly bodies and a life of immeasurable happiness—forever!

Thank You, Lord God, for giving me assurance of an eternal and meaningful life in heaven.

Find Your Strong Voice

A word spoken at the right time is like fruit of gold set in silver.

PROVERBS 25:11

Candy Lightner had never used her voice to stand up for politics or social reform, not until after May 3, 1980, when her daughter Cari was killed by a drunk driver. Thirteen-year-old Cari and a friend were walking to a church carnival when it happened. The driver who hit Cari never stopped. Enraged, Candy Lightner made a quick decision to take a stand against drunk driving. Four days after Cari died, her mother was already making plans. Soon she started the organization Mothers Against Drunk Driving (MADD) and later another nonprofit, We Save Lives. Since 1980, Candy Lightner has never stopped speaking out and fighting against impaired driving. Instead of expressing her anger in a useless word-filled rage, she channels it into something productive and good.[28]

Sometimes it takes a tragedy for us to find our strong voice and stand up for what we believe in. We live in a sinful world with much happening to fuel our anger. Today is the right time to find and use our voices to stand up, as God's people, for all that is good and right. What will you stand up for today?

Father, there is so much evil in the world today, so much to be angry about. Please give me strength to speak up for what is right. Guide me to be an advocate for others.

The Key to Resilience

In everything give thanks.
1 THESSALONIANS 5:18

Becky was experiencing what some might call a midlife crisis. The company she worked for moved its operations, leaving Becky unemployed. Shortly thereafter, Becky's father was diagnosed with Alzheimer's, and a few months later her mom died unexpectedly. In her late fifties, Becky was suddenly out of work and the sole caretaker for her dad. "Lord," she prayed, "help me!" At her mom's funeral, Becky's pastor gave her a book called *Find Hope When Life Hurts*. After praying one day, Becky picked up the book and began reading. A devotional about gratitude spoke to her. With her heart still aching, Becky thought of everything she had to be thankful for. The skills she'd learned in her job would transfer well if she decided to be self-employed or work part-time. She was grateful for years of wonderful memories of her mother and grateful that her dad still knew her. She was grateful to be a Christian and grateful for God. As she practiced gratitude, Becky's resilience grew, and she was more able to adapt to the difficulties she faced.

Life is hard sometimes. Maybe, like Becky, you are in the midst of adversity today. With God's help and a grateful heart, you can face your challenges and overcome them.

Oh Lord, with an aching but grateful heart I come to You today. Make me strong. Give me resilience to face and overcome my troubles.

In the Driver's Seat

"You call Me Teacher and Lord.
You are right because that is what I am."
JOHN 13:13

Heather disliked driving, especially on freeways. She gripped the steering wheel hard with both hands and never drove over the speed limit. Heart pounding, she'd pray again and again, "Jesus, *You* drive!" Believing Jesus was in control of her car gave Heather enough peace to continue on to her exit without having a full-blown panic attack. After a while, Heather became even more frightened to drive. She avoided the freeway altogether. The minute she got in her car, even to run short errands, she'd pray, "Jesus, *You* drive!" One day, to Heather's surprise, Jesus spoke to her heart, "No, Heather. You drive. I'll be sitting right next to you." As she thought about it, Heather decided she had always been a good and careful driver. She remembered the driving lessons she'd taken as a teenager and how confident and safe she'd felt with her instructor in the passenger seat. How much more confident would she be with Jesus sitting beside her?

When we are afraid, Jesus is not just our encourager and comforter but also our teacher. He teaches us to have confidence in our abilities and never lose sight that He is right there beside us—whatever we do and wherever we go.

Jesus, my Teacher and Lord, with You by my side I will gain confidence and conquer my fears. My trust is in You.

What Is True Love?

Love is patient, love is kind. It does not envy, it does not boast, it is not proud. It does not dishonor others, it is not self-seeking, it is not easily angered, it keeps no record of wrongs. Love does not delight in evil but rejoices with the truth. It always protects, always trusts, always hopes, always perseveres. Love never fails.

1 CORINTHIANS 13:4–8 NIV

Using just a few words, how would you define *love*? Dictionaries define *love* with phrases related to emotions: "a strong affection," "a warm attachment," "a benevolent concern for others." But love is more complex than warm, fuzzy feelings. Love can be lopsided. It can be disappointing and hurtful. Love requires tolerance, faith, and a healthy dose of understanding.

In 1 Corinthians 13, the apostle Paul tells us that true love is the display of selfless acts toward others. It is patience, kindness, humility, forgiveness, protection, trust, hopefulness, and perseverance. True love is the kind of love demonstrated to us by God, a faithful love that never fails.

When leaving our loved ones or saying goodbye on the phone, we casually say the words "I love you" and then the words drift away. A passionate love can sometimes grow cold. But perfect love, like God's love, doesn't change. It is forever unconditional, pure, and true.

Heavenly Father, teach me about true love. Lead me to love others not only through my words but also through my actions.

A Mother's Love

"The mountains may be taken away and the hills may shake, but My loving-kindness will not be taken from you. And My agreement of peace will not be shaken," says the Lord who has loving-pity on you.

ISAIAH 54:10

Baby Jackson was born with multiple cognitive and health issues. As a single mom, Ellen knew caring for Jackson would be a challenge, but she was determined to take her son home and provide him with around-the-clock care. As he got older, caring for Jackson became more difficult. Still, Ellen met his every need selflessly, diligently, and without complaining.

One day a friend asked, "How do you do it every day? You must be so tired." Ellen answered, "I love Jackson. Love gets me through—my love and God's." Ellen had learned to rely on God's compassionate love, believing that He would always give her strength. When her son screamed incessantly and Ellen didn't know what he wanted, God gave her strength. When she struggled to dress and change Jackson, God gave her strength to complete the task. Each night, Ellen thanked God for loving her through the day. Ellen's caring and determined disposition reminded others that if she could face her trials with strength, so could they by trusting in God's abiding love.

Lord, You know my troubles. I trust in Your love. I will rely on Your loving-kindness to give me strength and see me through.

There Are No Words

We do not know how to pray or what we should pray for, but the Holy Spirit prays to God for us with sounds that cannot be put into words.
ROMANS 8:26

There are times when we bow our heads to pray and the words won't come. "Dear God..." It could be we are exceedingly tired, overwhelmed with grief, or in such trouble that we just can't pray. Or maybe we are ashamed or angry and assume if we tell God how we really feel, He will punish us. Sometimes we just don't know what to say, worried that our words aren't eloquent enough for God's ears. God doesn't care how eloquent our words are. Without us telling Him, God already knows our thoughts. He cares about what's in our hearts. He wants to comfort us in our grief, help us through our troubles, and give us rest. He knows how we've sinned, and He wants to forgive us. When there are no words, the Holy Spirit prays to God for us.

When you pray, "Dear God," and the words won't come, sit quietly and wait. Perhaps God will give you the words to say, but if He doesn't, rest assured that the Holy Spirit will pray on your behalf. God knows exactly what you need. He hears you, and He loves you.

Dear God, You know what I want and what I need. Please help me to pray. I have no words.

Teach Us to Pray

Jesus had been praying. One of His followers said to Him, "Lord, teach us to pray."
LUKE 11:1

In the Lord's Prayer, Jesus teaches us how to pray. He begins, "Our Father in heaven, Your name is holy. May Your holy nation come. What You want done, may it be done on earth as it is in heaven" (Matthew 6:9–10). He first honors God, and then He continues, "Give us the bread we need today" (verse 11). This is where we submit our requests to God. Next, Jesus teaches us to seek God's forgiveness. "Forgive us our sins as we forgive those who sin against us" (verse 12). And finally, He leads us to ask God to protect us from Satan. "Do not let us be tempted but keep us from sin" (verse 13). The Lord's Prayer ends with Jesus once again recognizing God's power and sovereignty. "Your nation is holy. You have power and shining-greatness forever" (verse 13). When the words won't come and you don't know how to pray, try modeling your prayer using Jesus' example:

"Our Father in heaven, Your name is holy. May Your holy nation come. What You want done, may it be done on earth as it is in heaven. Give us the bread we need today. Forgive us our sins as we forgive those who sin against us. Do not let us be tempted, but keep us from sin. Your nation is holy. You have power and shining-greatness forever. [Amen]" (Matthew 6:9-13).

Cross My Heart

"For wherever your riches are, your heart will be there also."
MATTHEW 6:21

Finish this sentence with the first thing that comes to mind: "The most important thing in the world to me is. . ." Maybe you said "my children," "my spouse," or "my family." Those are the most common answers. Others are health, financial security, and safety. Some people answer with an activity or cause they are passionate about. But for those who love God, there is just one correct answer. The most important thing is God's gift of salvation. He sent His Son, Jesus, to die on the cross, sacrificing Himself and taking on our sins so that when we die, we can have all the riches God is holding for us in heaven.

The Bible says, "For wherever your riches are, your heart will be there also." God wants us to give our hearts to Jesus and put Him first, before anything else. God is the one who blesses us with children, spouses, family, and all the other things we love and find important. As we keep our hearts fixed on Him, He will continue to bless us abundantly. So thank God for His salvation and loving-kindness. Then use your blessings to honor Him.

Father God, You have blessed me so abundantly that sometimes I prioritize Your blessings above You. Keep reminding me that You are more important than anyone or anything else in my life. Everything I love and have comes from You.

Saying Goodbye

This is the reason we do not give up. Our human body is wearing out. But our spirits are getting stronger every day.
2 CORINTHIANS 4:16

When a loved one dies, the following prose poem by Luther F. Beecher can give us comfort and hope.

> *I am standing upon the seashore. A ship at my side spreads her white sails to the morning breeze, and starts for the blue ocean. She is an object of beauty and strength, and I stand and watch her until she hangs like a speck of white cloud just where the sea and sky come down to meet and mingle with each other. Then someone at my side says: "There! She's gone!" Gone where? Gone from my sight—that is all. She is just as large in mast and hull and spar as she was when she left my side, and just as able to bear her load of living freight to the place of her destination. Her diminished size is in me, and not in her. And just at that moment when someone at my side says, "There! She's gone!" there are other eyes that are watching for her coming; and other voices ready to take up the glad shout: "There she comes!" And that is—"dying."*[29]

The most difficult event we face on earth is the death of a loved one. Although we grieve, we find hope and comfort in God's promise of heaven.

Lord, welcome my loved one into Your open arms, and bless me with comfort and peace.

Go, Annie, Go!

Therefore encourage one another and build each other up, just as in fact you are doing.
1 THESSALONIANS 5:11 NIV

Annie's parents and friends eagerly awaited Annie's participation in her first Special Olympics. A swift runner, Annie had trained hard. Win or lose, she was determined to finish. Annie set her eyes on the finish line. Then—"Ready. Set. Go!" All along the track, Annie heard spectators shouting words of encouragement. "Go, Annie, go!" "You're almost there! "Annie, keep running!" She beamed as she crossed the finish line and fell into her coach's arms. "Good job, Annie!" he said. "I knew you could do it."

We all love hearing "Good job" and "I knew you could do it." But along with words, we encourage each other in many different ways. We look for what's good and strong in a person and celebrate it. We are encouraging and gentle when tolerating and forgiving someone's faults. We also can encourage others by recognizing their weaknesses and offering a helping hand. And we can always pray for someone and ask God to encourage them in ways we can't.

Everyone needs encouragement. Make it your mission to notice. Support others and cheer them on. Getting in the habit of being an encourager will bless others and you as well.

Dear God, let encouraging words be always on my lips. Please open my eyes to the needs of others and show me how I can provide encouragement and support.

When You Feel Discouraged

David encouraged himself in the Lord his God.

1 Samuel 30:6 KJV

First Samuel 30:1–6 tells of a time when David and his army went off to fight the Amalekites. Reluctantly, they had to leave their families behind. While they were gone, their enemy raided the city, burned it, and captured all the women and children. When the men returned, they found just a smoking pile of rubble. Furious and weeping uncontrollably, some blamed David and wanted him killed. What did David do when no one was around to encourage him? The Bible says he encouraged himself in the Lord.

David had an intimate relationship with God. He prayed constantly and had studied the scriptures. David relied on God's promises to encourage him in his time of need. In Psalm 119:15–16 (KJV) he says, "I will meditate in thy precepts, and have respect unto thy ways. I will delight myself in thy statutes: I will not forget thy word." Instead of wallowing in discouragement, David found strength and encouragement in his Lord. He had absolute trust in God's faithfulness.

We never have to face discouragement alone. When we trust God and recall the many times He has helped us through our troubles, we know He is always with us and always ready to lift us up.

Lord, thank You for encouraging me and building me up, especially when others are against me and I feel all alone.

Love Your Neighbor

Forget about the wrong things people do to you, and do not try to get even. Love your neighbor as you love yourself. I am the LORD.

LEVITICUS 19:18 NCV

Fred Rogers is well known for the way he encouraged kindness. The characters in his TV show *Mister Rogers' Neighborhood* were kind and caring neighbors. Wouldn't it be wonderful if neighbors always got along? But in reality, some neighbors aren't so neighborly.

Pete was that kind of neighbor. He kept to himself, often complained, and even called the police one afternoon when he thought the women next door laughed too loudly at their backyard baby shower. One day, that same next-door neighbor noticed Pete's overgrown lawn and overflowing mailbox. Upon learning that he had fallen, broken his leg, and was in the hospital, she and her husband did what good neighbors do. They cut Pete's grass, took in his mail, and visited him to see if there were other ways to help. Pete never did warm up to his neighbors, but still, they continued to treat him with kindness.

In Fred Rogers' words, "I think everybody longs to be loved, and longs to know that he or she is lovable."[30] Some people are hard to love, yet that is exactly what God commands of us—to love our neighbors.

Heavenly Father, teach me to love those who are difficult to love. Guide me to treat them with caring and kindness.

As the Sky Is High

O Lord, Your loving-kindness goes to the heavens.
You are as faithful as the sky is high.
PSALM 36:5

"In the beginning God created the heavens. . ." (Genesis 1:1 NIV). The immense space we call "the heavens" (or "sky") reaches far beyond what we can see or imagine. We find the sky mentioned throughout scripture. God set a rainbow there to promise a flood would never again destroy the earth. God used a myriad of stars in the sky to foretell Abraham's vast family. A single star heralded Christ's birth. Jesus told about the sky in the end times, saying, "There will be signs in the sun, moon, and stars. . . . Then people will see the Son of Man coming in a cloud with power and great glory" (Luke 21:25, 27 NCV).

In Psalm 19:1 David wrote, "The heavens are telling of the greatness of God and the great open spaces above show the work of His hands." Whenever we look up at the sky, we see God's works and wonder what lies beyond. God is there somewhere, bigger than anything we can imagine. His loving-kindness transcends the heavens. His faithfulness is as great as the sky is high.

Father, when I look up at the sky and pray, I'm in awe that my prayer travels far beyond the sky and into eternity where You are. You hear my prayers and provide for my needs. Great is Your faithfulness.

"You will know the truth and the truth will make you free."

JOHN 8:32

We live in a world rife with clashing viewpoints and criticisms. Headlines pull quotes out of context, facts are lost in opinions, and sometimes scripture is misquoted to promote a particular position or cause. How can we know the truth?

When Joyce pondered that question, she discovered that most of the time she agreed and disagreed with points made by both sides. Overall, that left her feeling unsettled. Joyce's mother was always a source of wisdom. When Joyce shared with her that she wasn't sure where she stood on the issues, her mom replied, "Dig deep. If ever there was a time to dig deep, it's now. Dig deep into scripture to be sure you haven't misunderstood God's words. Dig deep into your criticisms and feelings to determine if they are pleasing to God."

Joyce learned not to put too much faith in what others said. She did her best to get at the truth by deciding if her opinions agreed with God's Word. Before she decided to take a stand, she asked herself, "Would it please God?" When she dug deep, Joyce no longer felt unsettled. She knew the truth and it set her free.

Lord God, sometimes I'm uncertain which side I'm on, especially regarding some of the social issues we face today. Guide me to recognize when my opinions are pleasing to You and align with Your Word.

The Purpose of His Will

In him we were also chosen, having been predestined according to the plan of him who works out everything in conformity with the purpose of his will.

Ephesians 1:11 NIV

Officer Michael Michalski's funeral took place exactly one week after he was shot and killed while trying to make an arrest. The details of his murder aren't important. What's important is what God did next.

Officer Michalski, a born-again Christian, was saved five years before he died. Salvation had changed him from an angry man into someone who prayed for everyone he arrested. He knew he was a sinner just like them. Soon after his death, stories of Michalski's faith emerged. A video of his testimony at a local church began trending on social media. Local and national news media shared stories of his faith. Only God knows how many people were saved through personal encounters with Michalski and through his legacy.

It stormed the day of his funeral, but as the hearse carried Michalski's body to his grave, the rain stopped. God set a rainbow in the sky and the once angry, gray clouds broke apart and formed the shape of angel wings.[31]

We don't always understand why tragedies happen, but we know that God can pick up the pieces and reshape them into something beautiful.

Dear Father, thank You for putting together the shattered pieces of our lives to renew us and transform our darkness into light according to Your plan.

Warning: Danger!

The wise see danger ahead and avoid it,
but fools keep going and get into trouble.
PROVERBS 22:3 NCV

In the iconic film *A Christmas Story*, young Ralphie Parker wants a Red Ryder air rifle for Christmas. "You'll shoot your eye out!" his mom warns. *A Christmas Story* is set sometime around 1940. Times were different then. Most boys played with air rifles, cap guns, and fake grenades. On Independence Day, they set off Black Cat firecrackers, cherry bombs and M-80s—*boom!* Toys back then came with few, if any, warnings, and fireworks weren't banned.

Today we are inundated with warnings. "Caution: Contents hot!" "Warning: Small parts." "Keep away from children and pets." "Poison!" "Danger!" Almost everything we buy, and some things we do, comes with a warning. But have you noticed one very important warning is missing? It's the most important and lifesaving warning of all: "Stop! Not Knowing Jesus Can Result in Death."

In this dangerous time we live in, having a relationship with Jesus provides us with the wisdom to recognize the danger of sin and steer clear of it. Although there is no guarantee that physical harm can't touch us, the gift of salvation from Jesus gives us the assurance that nothing can ever destroy our souls.

Lord Jesus, I find solace in knowing that my soul is secure with You. Open my eyes to the dangers around me. Grant me wisdom and strength.

Coffee Talk

Perfume and incense bring joy to the heart, and the pleasantness of a friend springs from their heartfelt advice.

PROVERBS 27:9 NIV

"Would you like to meet for coffee?" Whether it's hot or iced, a cappuccino, latte, or traditional cup of coffee—black or with sugar and cream—there's something comfortable and familiar about meeting with friends in a coffee shop. Look around, and you will see most people engaged in conversation. If you listen closely, you might hear some serious discussions going on.

Rita and Monique met for coffee one Sunday as they usually did after church. Their pastor's sermon that day was about raising godly children. As they discussed the sermon, Monique, with tears in her eyes, confided that her teenaged son had gotten into some trouble along with his friends. Rita had experienced a similar issue with her son, and she was able to offer Monique solid, godly advice about what to do.

Women need other women. Firm, Christ-centered friendships lift us up when we're down, help us solve our problems, and often provide understanding when no one else "gets us." There is power in a godly friendship. It helps us stay centered on God's goodness and gives us courage to push on. Look to the women God has placed in your life. Who are your godly friends?

Lord, thank You for friends who understand, encourage, and support me. Bless them and keep them forever in Your care.

Take a Stand

Open your mouth. Be right and fair in what you decide. Stand up for the rights of those who are suffering and in need.
PROVERBS 31:9

Kaylee was furious that a dangerous incident at her child's high school hadn't been reported to parents. She'd heard from her daughter what happened and talked with another mom who had heard it from her children. "We need to do something," Kaylee said. "I'm afraid to get involved," the other mom replied, "These days, we have to be careful." Kaylee wasn't afraid to speak to the school's principal. Not satisfied with the principal's response, Kaylee went to the school board. As a result of her efforts, the board revised the district's methods for notifying parents.

While Proverbs 31:9 advises us to stand up for the rights of others, sometimes fear gets in the way—fear of the consequences, being judged, or becoming an outcast. Still, we should stand for what we know is good, fair, and right with God. Ephesians 6:13-14 tells us to "put on all the things God gives you to fight with. Then you will be able to stand in that sinful day. When it is all over, you will still be standing. So stand up and do not be moved."

Heavenly Father, thank You for giving me courage to stand up as an advocate for others and for everything that is good, right, and fair.

A Constant Companion

"And I am with you always, even to the end of the world."
MATTHEW 28:20

In 1892, C. Austin Miles, author of the hymn "In the Garden," gave up his job as a pharmacist to pursue a career writing gospel music. One day while reading his Bible, Miles pondered John 20:14–17, in which Mary Magdalene visits Jesus' tomb, finds it empty, and then sees Jesus standing there. "Jesus said to her, 'Mary!' She turned around and said to Him, 'Teacher!' Jesus said to her, 'Do not hold on to Me. I have not yet gone up to My Father'" (verses 16–17). Miles imagined himself there in the garden witnessing the event and recognized that as Christians we have constant companionship with our Lord. Later, he penned these words that became the hymn:

He speaks, and the sound of His voice
Is so sweet the birds hush their singing;
And the melody that He gave to me
Within my heart is ringing.
And He walks with me, and He talks with me,
And He tells me I am His own,
And the joy we share as we tarry there,
None other has ever known.[32]

Jesus is walking with you today and always. He hears you and talks with you. He says you are His—now and forever.

Dear Jesus, thank You for Your constant companionship and for loving me today and always.

Share the Good News

For I am not ashamed of the gospel, because it is the power of God that brings salvation to everyone who believes.

ROMANS 1:16 NIV

Although the Bible instructs us to share the gospel, some Christians find it difficult. They aren't sure what to say or how and when to say it. Actually, sharing the good news about Jesus isn't that hard. If you pray about it, the Lord will guide you.

With her friends and coworkers, Jackie led up to serious discussions about Jesus and salvation by first incorporating smaller "bites" into her conversations. When it felt right, she would casually interject phrases like, "I was just thinking about that last night while I was praying." Or "I'm so grateful that God blessed me with. . ." Or "That situation reminds me of ________________ in the Bible." She found she was able to lead more people to Christ by taking a slow, soft approach while patiently waiting for God to tell her when the moment was right to share the good news.

There are many different ways of sharing the gospel. Pray and ask God to lead you. Add Jesus to your conversations and keep it simple. Never allow fear to get in your way. Trust that God will give you the right words to say.

Lord God, help me to lead others to Christ. Make me aware of opportunities to share the gospel, and show me the way.

Ripple Effect

So My Word which goes from My mouth will not return to Me empty. It will do what I want it to do, and will carry out My plan well.

ISAIAH 55:11

Sharing God's Word is like throwing a rock into calm water. The bigger the rock, the bigger the splash. Then energy from the splash causes a ripple as the water tries to spread out the energy. When we share God's Word with others, and then they share it, a similar ripple effect happens. We can't know how far the ripple extends or how many people it reaches, but God promises His Word will do what He wants it to do.

The Bible is the best example of the ripple effect. Written thousands of years ago, the Word of God continues to be the most read book in the world with billions of copies sold. The words of the Bible are God-inspired and have been handed down from generation to generation.

Sometimes we are blessed to see the results of sharing God's Word—someone being led to salvation or helped through a crisis in life. Often, however, we don't know the effect that sharing His Word has. We can be sure, though, that the words we share will not return to God empty. He will use them to carry out His plan.

Father, as I share Your Word with others, may it serve to encourage them and lead them closer to You.

Pray Big

God is able to do much more than we ask or think through His power working in us.

Ephesians 3:20

Fran cherished time spent with her granddaughter Carrie. Next year, Carrie would graduate from high school and go away to college. "I really want to be a veterinarian," Carrie told her grandmother, "but I think I'll just study to be a vet technician." "Why not a vet?" Fran asked. "Because the program is long and hard," Carrie answered, "and, well, I just don't think I could do it." "Yes, you can!" Fran replied. "If God put it in your heart to be a veterinarian, He will give you the power to get there." Fran knew if Carrie didn't try to reach her goal, she might regret it later in life.

Jabez was a man who prayed big. He knew God was able to give Him even more than he wanted. "Jabez cried out to the God of Israel, 'Oh, that you would bless me and enlarge my territory!' . . . And God granted his request" (1 Chronicles 4:10 NIV). When we pray big, we open the door for God to do even more than we imagine. When we ask Him for big things, we exercise our faith. It's not so much about the outcome as it is about acknowledging and trusting that God can do infinitely more than we ask.

Oh God, open my eyes to the possibilities. Bless me with even more than I ask.

I Believe

The eyes of those who do not believe are made blind by Satan who is the god of this world. He does not want the light of the Good News to shine in their hearts.

2 CORINTHIANS 4:4

Merriam-Webster defines *believe* as simply accepting the word or evidence of something.[33] But then it goes further to define the phrase *believe in*—to have faith or confidence in the existence of (something); to have trust in the goodness or value of (something); to have trust in the goodness or ability of (someone).[34] *Believe*. One simple word. But when we believe in the existence of God, in His goodness, and in His ability, then the word packs immeasurable power.

Satan wants to take that power away. He loves the word *doubt*. Satan wants us to doubt God's goodness, His ability, and especially His existence. Satan loves telling us, "If God is good, why does He allow bad things to happen? If God is able, why doesn't He stop them from happening? Maybe God doesn't exist at all." When we believe Satan's words, we lose our power to resist him. Especially in difficult times, it's important to hold tightly to our belief in God and trust in His goodness. When we firmly believe and are not shaken, then His power will flow through us.

Lord God, I believe You exist as the one and only true God. I believe in Your goodness, Your ability, and Your power working within me.

Peace in God

But I am calm and quiet, like a baby with its mother.
I am at peace, like a baby with its mother.
PSALM 131:2 NCV

David was far from perfect. He committed adultery with Bathsheba, who became pregnant with his child, and then arranged the murder of Bathsheba's husband. David was a sinner. He confessed his sins to God, and God forgave him, but still David had to live with the consequences of his sins. In his life, he had trouble. His baby with Bathsheba died. David's adult sons had issues. (Amnon was guilty of rape and incest. Absalom murdered Amnon and tried to overthrow David as king.) But perhaps the most well-known of David's troubles was when David became a fugitive while fleeing Saul, who wanted to kill him. In all his troubles, David repented of his sins and found peace in his relationship with God. He found peace by trusting in God's love and fully committing himself to God's will. Finding peace in God strengthened David's faith, and God led him to do great things.

God gives us power to overcome our sins. When we confess our sins to God and repent, we can find perfect peace by accepting His forgiveness and trusting in His goodness. "The LORD gives strength to his people; the LORD blesses his people with peace" (Psalm 29:11 NCV).

Heavenly Father, forgive me for my sins. Help me to find peace in Your forgiveness and in Your infinite love for me.

Our Shepherd's Voice

For as he thinks in his heart, so is he.

Proverbs 23:7

Kay noticed that her coworker Sandra was unusually quiet. She brought her a cup of coffee and asked, "Is everything all right?" "I don't know," Sandra answered. "I can't seem to say the right things to my kids or do anything right. Sometimes I wonder if they even love me." Clearly, Sandra had been listening to Satan's lies and believed them. Satan likes to condemn. He enjoys speaking put-downs into our hearts as he tries to drown out the Lord's voice.

In John 10:27 Jesus says, "My sheep hear My voice and I know them. They follow Me." When we learn to distinguish our Shepherd's voice from any other voices speaking inside our hearts, then we will know the truth. Jesus will never say that we are worthless, that we can't do anything right, or that nobody loves us. His voice is gentle but firm. He builds us up, encourages us, and never puts us down. Our Lord's voice will never contradict God's Word. So sit quietly, ask Him to speak to you, and then listen for His voice. Ask Jesus to put in your mind all the good things that make you *you*.

Lord Jesus, guide me to recognize Your voice, the voice of truth, speaking within my heart. Lead me away from believing Satan's lies. Strengthen and empower me to resist him when he speaks.

Build a Godly Home

A house is built by wisdom. It is made strong by understanding, and by much learning the rooms are filled with all riches that are pleasing and of great worth.

PROVERBS 24:3–4

How do we create godly homes? By building strong foundations. Our heavenly Father is the master builder, and the Bible is His blueprint. When we seek wisdom in His Word and apply it to our households, God will help us establish firm foundations to build on.

A godly home is one in which God comes first—even before our husbands and kids. It is a safe place where all family members feel accepted, understood, honored, and loved. It is where parents and children pray with and for each other and praise and worship God. The walls of a godly home are so strong that nothing can penetrate them. It is where God teaches parents how to parent and where children learn to honor their parents and love the Lord. It is a place of forgiveness, grace, and unconditional love. A godly home isn't a perfect home. We will face obstacles that require revisiting the blueprint, but when we trust in the Master Builder, He will help us overcome whatever gets in our way.

Dear God, I want our home to be a godly home, a home blessed by Your presence. Be the head of our household. Guide us to build our home on the foundation of Your Word.

Recharge Me

I will lie down and sleep in peace. O Lord, You alone keep me safe.
PSALM 4:8

When the batteries run low on our phones and other devices, we recharge them. Without charging, these gadgets lose their power to help us function. Isn't it odd that we are attentive to recharging our devices but not so vigilant to recharge our bodies and minds?

Maybe you lie awake at night with your mind racing. There's something about turning off the light and lying in bed that puts our thoughts into overdrive. We revisit the day's events and think about tomorrow, and sometimes we worry. We look at the clock and see that one hour, two hours, or more have ticked by. We know that with less sleep we won't be as sharp or ready to function when the alarm goes off in the morning.

David discovered how to get a peaceful night's sleep. He gave all his thoughts and troubles to the Lord. David understood that while he slept, God was working His perfect plan to take care of everything David worried about. When he lay there thinking about the Lord, sleep came easily to David.

What will your thoughts be like when you lie down tonight? Give them to God. If you allow Him to calm your restless thoughts, you will awake recharged and ready for the day.

Lord, tonight I surrender all my thoughts to You. Grant me peaceful sleep as I rest in the safety of Your love.

He Chose Me

"You have not chosen Me, I have chosen you. I have set you apart for the work of bringing in fruit."
JOHN 15:16

"I chose to follow Jesus." You might hear similar words when someone gives their testimony. Following the Lord is a wonderful, life-changing decision. But the truth is, we don't choose Him—He chooses us! God has a plan for everyone. He puts us on earth to bear fruit. That means to bring Him glory through everything we say and do. When we abide in Jesus and work toward having character attributes like His, we bring glory to God. When we add more love, joy, peace, and patience into the world, we bear fruit.

Jesus chooses us to be His disciples. He sets us apart from the rest of the world with the purpose of doing His work. Our mission is to use our skills and talents to serve Him, to cultivate a character like His, to treat others as He would treat them, and especially to lead others to salvation. He has chosen you to be His. He gave you life and a purpose. You are an integral part of His plan, and He wants you to represent Him here on earth. Do your best every day to bring Him glory in all that you do.

Dear Jesus, thank You for choosing me as Your disciple. Lead me to bear fruit that brings honor and glory to God.

Come and Hear

"Listen and come to Me. Hear, so you may live. And I will make an agreement with you that lasts forever."

ISAIAH 55:3

Sally searched for answers. Her life was a mess, and although she desired to fix it, she couldn't. She sat alone in a coffee shop, playing a video game on her phone, when she heard a voice address a woman sitting by herself at a nearby table, "Good morning, Pastor." "Good morning," the pastor replied. Then the woman went back to drinking her coffee and reading her Bible. Something led Sally to speak to her. "Good morning," she said. "Nice day, isn't it?" The two women exchanged small talk, and soon the pastor invited Sally to sit with her. Before long, Sally was telling the pastor all her troubles. "Let's pray about it," the pastor said. After they prayed, she told Sally about Jesus and His gift of eternal life. Sally was saved that morning in the coffee shop, and her life changed forever.

God wants everyone to have eternal life in heaven. Listen when He leads you to share the gospel. Don't let an opportunity pass you by. It could change a life forever.

Dear God, how many chances have I missed to lead someone to Christ? Please make me more aware of opportunities to share the gospel. When You nudge me to speak to a stranger or make a new friend, remind me to listen and obey.

Talking with God

I call to God; God will help me. At dusk, dawn, and noon I sigh deep sighs—he hears, he rescues.

PSALM 55:17 MSG

How would you describe your prayer life? Are there specific times when you pray? Morning, mealtime, and bedtime prayers are common. But what about all-the-time prayers? God is waiting to talk with us at dawn, noon, dusk and every time in between. He goes wherever we go, and He wants us to include Him in our thoughts all day. Do you praise God for giving you the skill and strength to complete a difficult task? Do you ask Him to guide you before an important meeting with your boss? Do you thank Him for keeping you safe after a close call on the highway?

God loves you. Like any parent, He wants to help you and keep you from getting into trouble. But unlike any parent, He is able to be with you 100 percent of the time. He hears your sighs when you feel frustrated, and He hears your calls for help. Get in the habit of talking silently with God all day long. It will make you more aware of His constant presence and His willingness to help.

Heavenly Father, I often get so caught up in life that I forget You are always with me. I will try to talk to You more throughout the day and listen for Your voice in my heart.

Teach Your Children Well

Be careful to listen to all these words I am telling you. Then it will go well with you and your children after you forever.

DEUTERONOMY 12:28

In Proverbs 22:6 (KJV) Solomon wrote, "Train up a child in the way he should go: and when he is old, he will not depart from it." For parents this means knowing God's Word, applying it at home, and setting a godly example.

Some parents have grown up in homes that weren't so godly, and they've carried that bad example into adulthood and are passing it along to their children. But if they choose to study the Bible and put its words into action, they can turn their ungodly home into a God-centered home.

A home rich in God's wisdom and presence is one where children learn to do what is good and right in the eyes of the Lord. Their parents want a godly character to be their children's inheritance—they want to believe in and trust God, to live in ways that please Him, and to pass that heritage along to their children. God doesn't ask us to be perfect, but He does expect us to do our best to obey and honor Him and teach our children to do the same.

Oh God, how I want my children to know and love You. Lead me as I teach them to obey and respect You and to live their lives to please You.

I Am Woman!

Let the weakling say, "I am strong!"
JOEL 3:10 NIV

Singer and songwriter Helen Reddy attributed the inspiration for her 1970s hit "I Am Woman" to the strong women in her family who had survived the Great Depression and two world wars.[35] Throughout history, strong women have always inspired others. For example, in the Bible, Queen Esther saved a nation. Empowered by God, Judge Deborah made wise decisions and showed bravery and strength as a warrior and military leader. Then there was Mary, the mother of Jesus, who God had decided was strong and brave enough to give birth to and raise His Son. And Anna, the prophetess who persevered in waiting patiently for the Lord.

God created women to be strong. He gave us the strength to give birth to our children, the wisdom to discern and solve problems, the bravery to meet tough challenges, the talents and skills required to lead, the patience and understanding needed to teach, and the faith to stand against all our troubles. And added to all that is physical strength to become great athletes and creativity to paint, make music, dance, and more. All of our abilities come from God, King of the universe.

Think about the strong women in your family. What made them strong? How has their strength inspired you?

Father God, when I am weak, You give me strength. Pour Your mighty power into me. Make me strong so together we can do great things.

It's a New Day

The Lord within her is right and good. He will be fair and do nothing wrong. Every morning He brings to light what is fair. Every new day He is faithful.

ZEPHANIAH 3:5

It's a new day! Aren't you glad? While you slept, God was working on yesterday's troubles. Today, you can begin by putting all your faith and trust in Him and asking Him to guide you. Today, you can apply what you learned from yesterday's mistakes, you can make amends or forgive someone for yesterday's transgressions, and you can put yesterday's failures in the past and try again. Today, you can shift your thoughts from negative to positive, stay in the present, and allow God to lead you. You can challenge yourself to walk a bit farther toward your goals, to be open to new experiences and opportunities, to align your thoughts and opinions with God's Word, and to become a better representative for Christ.

Today, as a child of God, you are alive, blessed, forgiven, loved, accepted, and chosen. God created you, and He made this day for you to live to the fullest. So embrace this day! Do what is right, good, and fair—and above all, thank God and praise Him for His faithfulness.

Lord God, thank You for this new day! Walk with me, talk with me, and guide me. Make me aware of all the opportunities to make today a good day.

A Broken Friendship

My confusion is continually before me,
and the shame of my face hath covered me.
Psalm 44:15 KJV

Lisa was guilty. No mistake about it. Her best friend, Eileen, had shared something with Lisa in confidence, and Lisa had told a mutual friend. Then everything blew up. That friend whom Lisa had trusted told **her** friend, and she told a friend, and. . .Eileen's secret went viral. Lisa and Eileen's friendship was broken, and so was their bond of trust. Lisa felt ashamed. She wanted Eileen's friendship back and whole, as it used to be. But she was confused about what to do.

When trust is broken, sometimes a simple apology is not enough to mend it. It takes two to mend a relationship. When Lisa apologized to Eileen, she was sincere. She asked Eileen to forgive her and promised not to make the same mistake again. Eileen wasn't ready to jump back into their friendship, so Lisa stepped aside after telling Eileen that she loved her and she hoped that somehow their friendship could be restored.

Repairing a broken relationship often requires space, time, patience, and prayer, as well as a release of the entire situation to God. Where there is love, forgiveness is possible. The God of our hope makes all things possible.

Lord God, I was at fault. Please forgive me.
Free me from these feelings of guilt and shame.
I ask that You take this broken relationship and
make it whole again. I surrender it into Your hands.

The Cluttered Heart

The heart is free where the Spirit of the Lord is.
2 CORINTHIANS 3:17

If you've ever watched the television show *Hoarders*, then you understand the true meaning of the word *clutter*. People can hold on to so many things that their lives become unmanageable. It becomes impossible to decide what is most important to hang on to and what can be let go, so they just move things around until there's no place to put them anymore.

The same can be true of our hearts. When our minds fill up with stuff, it overflows into our hearts. Worrisome thoughts, grievances, work issues, relationship problems, responsibilities, to-do lists. . . Guilt and shame for our sins end up there too, usually at the bottom of the pile so we don't have to deal with them. Before long, our hearts become so cluttered with stuff that there's no room for Jesus.

Second Corinthians 3:17 says, "The heart is free where the Spirit of the Lord is." The only way to free our hearts is to get rid of all the unnecessary stuff and allow Him to fill the empty space with His Spirit. Think about it. Is there stuff in your heart you can get rid of to make more room for Him?

Dear Jesus, tell me what I need to get rid of to make more space in my heart for You.

Me Too!

Tell your sins to each other. And pray for each other so you may be healed. The prayer from the heart of a man right with God has much power.

James 5:16

Anxiously, Kayla entered the place where the Alcoholics Anonymous meeting was held. She sat quietly in the back. The meeting had begun, and a short, dark-skinned woman stood speaking to the group. "My drinking almost cost me my husband and children, but God rescued me. Believe me, there is hope." The woman's words stung. When Kayla drank, she neglected her children's needs. Just that morning, her oldest daughter had told her so. It was time to do something about her addiction.

After the meeting, Kayla approached the woman, who then invited Kayla to have coffee. "I'm an alcoholic," the woman shared. "Me too," Kayla whispered. "I'm also a Christian," the woman added. "Me too," said Kayla. So began a friendship made in heaven. God had led Kayla to this woman so she could lead Kayla to sobriety.

Sometimes confessing our faults to one another leads to a "me too" moment that unleashes the power of God to right what is wrong. Maybe you know of someone facing a problem you once faced. Sharing your experience of how God helped you might be just what she needs to begin the healing process.

Father, show me how sharing the problems I've overcome can be a source of help to others.

Come with Me

[Jesus] said to them, "Come with me by yourselves to a quiet place and get some rest."
MARK 6:31 NIV

Jesus had sent out His twelve disciples, two by two, into the nearby villages to tell the people that they should repent. Jesus also gave them authority to cast out demons and heal the sick. The disciples worked hard and returned to Jesus exhausted. The crowds had been so big the disciples hadn't even had time to eat. Jesus said to them, "Come with me by yourselves to a quiet place and get some rest."

Imagine feeling so tired from working so hard and hearing Jesus say to you, "Come with Me by yourself and get some rest." Wouldn't that be wonderful? But you don't have to imagine it. Jesus is saying to us right now, "Come to me, all you who are weary and burdened, and I will give you rest" (Matthew 11:28 NIV). Jesus is our safe place, our quiet place, and our place of peace. When we take time to be still, pray, and give our worries to Him, then we are at rest with Him.

Quiet your soul before Jesus today. Meditate on His love and constant presence. When you are weary, you can trust Him to care for you, calm you, and renew your strength.

Dear Jesus, I am so tired. Please lead me to that quiet place where we can rest for a while.

With Wings Like Eagles

But they who wait upon the Lord will get new strength. They will rise up with wings like eagles. They will run and not get tired. They will walk and not become weak.

Isaiah 40:31

When observing eagles in flight, you may have noticed that unlike many other birds, they soar without flapping their wings much. Eagles were designed by God to depend on air currents, called updrafts, to stay aloft. This characteristic allows them to conserve energy and effortlessly glide at heights of up to 10,000 feet without becoming weary from constant wing flapping.[36]

The prophet Isaiah compared the strength we get from the Lord to the way eagles soar. The strength that comes from God allows us to keep going without becoming weary and weak. Isaiah's message was directed to the Israelites during a time of captivity. It encouraged them to wait with patience and hope for the Lord to come and lift them out of their troubles. Isaiah's message is for us too. In troubling times, when we've done all that we can do, we know that God will come for us. We can trust in Him while we wait. And when He comes, He will give us new strength to leave our troubles behind and carry on.

Heavenly Father, I patiently wait for You. Please lift me up on wings like an eagle and let me soar above my troubles. My hope and trust are in You.

Battle Scars

Let your minds and hearts be made new.
EPHESIANS 4:23

Life is a battle of wills, and sometimes we lose. Few of us get through life without scars. Our bodies have scars from old injuries. Our minds and hearts have scars too—old hurts, bad decisions, failures, missed opportunities. We can hide the scars on our bodies with clothing and makeup. Scars of the mind and heart we hide with our actions and attitudes. But the good news is we don't have to hide our scars. Jesus' death on the cross and His resurrection make it possible for every one of our sins to be forgiven and our wounds to be healed. Instead of hiding our scars with regret, we can proudly display them as battle scars, a symbol of our victory over sin through Jesus.

We have a Savior who loves us so much that He endured great suffering so that we wouldn't have to. According to Isaiah 53:5, Jesus "was hurt for our wrong-doing. He was crushed for our sins. He was punished so we would have peace. He was beaten so we would be healed." Embrace His gift of healing today. Consider your scars as battle scars, a reminder of the troubles you've overcome. Let your heart and mind be renewed.

Lord Jesus, thank You for loving me so deeply that You suffered and died for my sins. Thank You for healing my wounds and renewing my heart and mind.

Take Hold

Brothers and sisters, I do not consider myself yet to have taken hold of it. But one thing I do: Forgetting what is behind and straining toward what is ahead, I press on toward the goal to win the prize for which God has called me heavenward in Christ Jesus.

PHILIPPIANS 3:13–14 NIV

In her late teens, Marcie's path took an unexpected turn when she fell in love with a soldier and left college to marry him. Decades later, with grown children and a wealth of life experience, Marcie felt it was time to pursue her long-held dream. As the oldest student in her classes at a local college, she was happy to be accepted by her younger peers, and she engaged in lively conversations with them in the college cafeteria. When asked about her decision to drop out at age nineteen, Marcie shared that she had fallen in love. When questioned if she regretted her decision, she answered, "I don't regret it; instead, I forget it. Right now I'm solely focused on my future—achieving my goal of earning a degree."

Maybe, like Marcie, you have an old goal you'd still like to reach. You can regret, for the rest of your life, the dream you didn't follow, or you can take hold of it, as Paul says, "straining toward what is ahead." Which will you choose?

Heavenly Father, there's a goal I've wanted to pursue for a very long time. Is it time to follow my dream, or do You have a different plan for me? Please lead me in the direction I should go.

Time for a Checkup

Let us test and look over our ways, and return to the Lord.

LAMENTATIONS 3:40

When it's time to make an appointment for our annual physical, it isn't something we look forward to. Still, we know a checkup is important for our body's health. A checkup includes a thorough examination and often tests. Sometimes everything checks out fine. Other times there is room for improvement.

In Lamentations 3:40, Jeremiah was urging God's people to submit to a different kind of checkup. He wanted them to take a good, hard look inside their hearts and test for the sins lurking there. We all have sin inside our hearts. Romans 3:23 (KJV) says, "For all have sinned, and come short of the glory of God." We all need a thorough self-examination to be aware of whether we are living in ways that please the Lord. When we discover sin in ourselves, the remedy is found in Romans 3:24 (NCV): "All need to be made right with God by his grace, which is a free gift." When we confess our sins to God and repent, then we are made right through His grace and freed from our sins.

Take time today to test yourself. Is there room for improvement?

Father God, I desire to live in a way that pleases You. I will search my heart and seek forgiveness for my sins, knowing that Your grace will make me righteous in Your sight.

The Talk

How can a young person live a pure life? By obeying your word.
PSALM 119:9 NCV

Joan and Gary raised their children to have strong Christian values. They did their best to model Christlike behavior and to teach their children to do the same. Still, when they sent their oldest son off to college, they worried about the environment he would be in. He would be subject to values unlike his own, and he would form new relationships, some with peers who held viewpoints in conflict with his. Joan and Gary hoped they had prepared him well enough to face these new challenges.

All parents face the day when their child graduates from high school and steps into adulthood. The teen years are a great time for parents to have "the talk" with their children about how to defend their faith. First Peter 3:15 says, "Always be ready to tell everyone who asks you why you believe as you do. Be gentle as you speak and show respect." Joan and Gary had conversations with their son about how he might respond if his faith was challenged. As they sent him off to college, they felt assured that they had done their best to prepare him to leave home without leaving his faith behind.

Lord God, please help me prepare my children for adulthood. Help me guide them to always defend their faith and to live a pure life according to Your Word.

Lost and Found

Now Isaac's servants dug in the valley and found a well of flowing water there.
GENESIS 26:19

We can think of the "living water" mentioned in the Bible as water that is constantly fresh and flowing. It quenches our thirst and refreshes us on our journey through life. This living water is a metaphor for Jesus and the spiritual sustenance, or help, He provides us through the Holy Spirit.

In Genesis 26:19 we find another metaphor: Isaac's servants digging in a valley and finding there a well of flowing water. There are times when we walk through spiritual valleys in our lives where we can't seem to find help. When we are thirsty and in need of living water, finding it might require digging deep inside our hearts until we find Jesus there. He is always with us in the valleys of our lives, ready to give us rest and refreshment so we can grow stronger. He sends us the Holy Spirit, who is present in the valleys just as much as on the mountaintops, clearing a path for us to navigate through our challenges. When Jesus and the living water He provides seem far away, remember that they are not! They are present inside your heart. Keep digging until you find them.

Jesus, You seem so far away. I know You are with me inside my heart, so please help me find You. I need Your living water to sustain me and help me through this valley.

Martha, Martha!

Jesus said to her, "Martha, Martha, you are worried and troubled about many things. Only a few things are important, even just one."
LUKE 10:41–42

During His travels, Jesus would occasionally stay at the home of his good friends, sisters Mary and Martha. Once while Jesus was visiting, Mary sat at His feet, listening to everything He said. Meanwhile, Martha was busy preparing supper. She went to Jesus and said, "Lord, don't you care that my sister has left me to do the work by myself? Tell her to help me!" Jesus replied, "Martha, Martha, . . . you are worried and upset about many things, but few things are needed—or indeed only one. Mary has chosen what is better, and it will not be taken away from her" (Luke 10:39–42 NIV). Martha was so preoccupied with serving Jesus that she forgot the importance of focusing on His teachings.

Jesus tells us it is essential to fix our thoughts on Him. Yes, serving Him and others is good, but even more important is sitting at His feet in the intimacy of His presence, forsaking all distractions in our relationship with Him. Our utmost priority should be staying present with Jesus and listening to and learning from Him.

Lord Jesus, I ask Your forgiveness for allowing my own desires to overshadow my relationship with You. Today and always, I will do my best to prioritize sitting at Your feet, focused on You above all else.

The Power of Words

Words kill, words give life;
they're either poison or fruit—you choose.
PROVERBS 18:21 MSG

The American novelist Nathaniel Hawthorne is credited with saying, "Words—so innocent and powerless as they are, as standing in a dictionary, how potent for good and evil they become in the hands of one who knows how to combine them."[37] Our words have power to lift up or tear down. That is why we should always use them to exemplify God's Word.

Just as important as the words we use are the ways we say them. Words congruent with God's Word are true, wise, firm, and fair. They are offered in kind, gentle, and caring ways. When they need to be firm, they are said with respect. They never lie. They strive to lift up and not tear down. The words we use should never contradict God's Word or lead others away from it. Our words should always honor God and be pleasing to Him. Things like anger, frustration, jealousy, and disappointment can poison our words, but we have the power to keep them from passing through our lips. Knowing how to combine words so they lead to goodness takes practice, but by thinking before we speak and asking God for help, we can do it.

Father God, I am guilty of letting unkind words slip out of my mouth. Forgive me. Help me to think before I speak and always use my words to honor You.

Surprise—You're in Charge!

"Get up, for this is your duty, but we will be with you. Have strength of heart and do it."
EZRA 10:4

Shirley casually mentioned to her Bible study group, "I wish our church had a fall festival. It would be a great way to invite others to visit our church." Several days later, Shirley received a call from her pastor who had learned of her great idea. "I think it's a wonderful idea," he said. "Let's do it! You're in charge." Shirley's heart sank. A wave of fear rushed through her. She had never been in charge of anything, and a festival was a big deal. She didn't know if she could do it, so she prayed and asked God for help.

Maybe, like Shirley, you have been in the position of unexpectedly being put in charge. How did you handle it? You likely discovered that you were not alone. Others came to help. With their help, you gained confidence, and the idea of leadership wasn't so frightening anymore.

Shirley's fall festival was a great success. She led it for several more years and then used her leadership skills to serve God in other ways. God works everything out for good for those who rely on Him. Is He guiding you to be a leader? Accept the challenge. Have strength of heart and do it.

Here I am, Lord. Give me wisdom to lead well, and provide me with the help I need.

Pray for Our Leaders

We always pray for you. We pray that our God will make you worth being chosen. We pray that His power will help you do the good things you want to do. We pray that your work of faith will be complete.

2 THESSALONIANS 1:11

As Christians, we seek leaders who follow God's Word and lead with godly principles. We want leaders chosen by God who will seek His guidance to carry out good works according to His will. The Bible instructs us to pray for our leaders: "Pray for kings and all others who are in power over us so we might live quiet God-like lives in peace. It is good when you pray like this. It pleases God Who is the One Who saves" (1 Timothy 2:2–3). Praying for our pastors, bosses, community leaders, government officials, and others is important, even if we disagree with them. We can pray for their salvation and that they would have wisdom, courage, and strength to rule faithfully and obediently. By praying in this way, we please God and experience His peace, knowing that He is ultimately in control. Add leaders to your daily prayer list and pray vigilantly for them. If you find it hard to pray for them, remember that your prayers bring glory to God.

Lord God, help me to pray for our leaders even when it's hard. May they seek Your guidance in all they do.

True Wealth

You might say to yourself, "I am rich because of my own power and strength," but remember the LORD your God! It is he who gives you the power to become rich.

DEUTERONOMY 8:17–18 NCV

In the musical *Fiddler on the Roof*, the character Tevye dreams of a life filled with wealth and respect. Despite his desire for material riches, Tevye has a deep connection with God. He essentially says to the Lord, "God, if I were rich and didn't have to work, I'd have more time to pray. Would it be so terrible if I were rich?"

True wealth isn't about material possessions. Our true riches come from God's enduring love for us. He blesses us with what we truly need—loving relationships, good health to enjoy life to the fullest, meaningful work, a safe home where we find comfort and rest—these are just several of His blessings. While money and possessions may bring temporary happiness, they don't last. Jesus said, "For where your treasure is, there your heart will be also" (Matthew 6:21 NIV). When we make God our priority, He blesses us beyond our imagination, enriching our lives with the kind of peace, comfort, and joy that can only be found in Him.

Heavenly Father, everything I have comes from You. You have provided me with riches that money cannot buy. I am deeply grateful for all You have done for me, and I thank You for Your abundant blessings.

Strength to Forgive

"If you forgive people their sins, your Father in heaven will forgive your sins also."
MATTHEW 6:14

Television shows like *48 Hours* and *20/20* have been popular for years. People are fascinated by true crime stories, perhaps because they desire less crime and more justice for the perpetrators. Sometimes viewers are taken inside the courtroom to hear victim impact statements in which family members are allowed to speak before a convicted criminal is sentenced. Many of these statements are angry and emotional, but a few offer forgiveness. Is it possible to say, "I forgive you," and mean it, to someone who has caused you such pain? Yes, if for no other reason than God commands it.

Forgiving someone of a heinous, life-shattering act takes a kind of strength only God can provide. Forgiving doesn't mean we forget what was done. Instead, it surrenders our anger to God, knowing He has power to convict the criminal in ways the court system cannot. God has power over the mind and heart. When we forgive, we release the wrongdoer into God's hands, allowing Him to work in the person's heart as He wills. We don't know who we will meet in heaven. God has the power to change even the coldest, hardest hearts. Forgiveness allows us to move forward with our lives, trusting that God has the situation under His control.

Father God, please give me strength.
Help me to forgive and release this terrible
wrongdoing into Your almighty hands.

A Time to Laugh

There is a time to cry, and a time to laugh;
a time to have sorrow, and a time to dance.
ECCLESIASTES 3:4

Immediately before he presented his Emancipation Proclamation and while waiting for a meeting with his cabinet members to begin, President Abraham Lincoln read an article written by General Artemas Ward. Lincoln found humor in the article, and he laughed as he read. Lincoln's Secretary of War, Edwin Stanton, didn't understand how the president could laugh in the midst of such a serious time. "With the fearful strain that is upon me night and day, if I did not laugh I should die," Lincoln told him.[38]

We're all familiar with the idiom, "Laughter is the best medicine." It's likely derived from Proverbs 17:22, "A glad heart is good medicine, but a broken spirit dries up the bones." Laughter is good for our souls. A little humor in difficult or stressful times can help to lighten the load. The Bible is clear that there is a time for us to laugh. While not always appropriate in solemn or somber situations, in most circumstances laughter can soften a tense situation and improve physical symptoms caused by stress. Allow yourself to laugh a little. It can't cure everything, but a chuckle or a hearty guffaw can make a trying situation easier to handle.

Dear Lord, during this stressful time, let my spirits be lifted by moments of laughter.

Make Him Proud

He gave the right and the power to become children of God to those who received Him. He gave this to those who put their trust in His name.

JOHN 1:12

As Adrienne reflected on her twenty-five years of marriage, she thanked God for her husband. Through the years of their marriage, Adrienne's list of Ralph's good qualities had grown. Above all, he was an excellent father. From the days their children were born, Ralph loved on them. He changed diapers and wiped away spit-up, and as they grew older, Ralph led them toward living good and godly lives. The kids were young adults now. Their love for the Lord, the work they had accomplished, and the goals they pursued made their papa proud. The kids made God proud too—proud of them and also of Ralph.

When we ponder the good qualities of our heavenly Father's character, we discover the list is infinite. God is loving, compassionate, caring, forgiving, and fair. He is our teacher, comforter, helper, and guide. We are His children, and He imparts to us many of His good attributes. God wants us to use them to make Him proud. What an incredible blessing it is to be called children of God and to be led by His Spirit toward living good and godly lives.

Father, I want You to be proud of the way I live my life. Please guide me.

A Gentle and Quiet Spirit

Your beauty should come from the inside. It should come from the heart. This is the kind that lasts. Your beauty should be a gentle and quiet spirit. In God's sight this is of great worth and no amount of money can buy it.

1 PETER 3:4

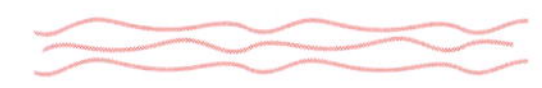

"She's so quiet." "Who?" "That new woman in church. The one who sits in the back on Sundays. She smiles and says hello, but she doesn't make an effort to know us."

Had they gotten to know her, they would have discovered Denise was someone with a gentle and quiet spirit. Shy and an introvert, she didn't often reach out to others, but if she saw someone in need, Denise was the first to be there with a kind and loving heart. She loved the Lord. She served Him quietly, but she served Him well.

The quiet people among us are sometimes overlooked or misjudged as aloof and unfriendly. But a quiet spirit might just reflect someone who is diffident and meek and who, in social situations, shrinks away from others. Jesus said, "Blessed are the meek: for they shall inherit the earth" (Matthew 5:5 KJV). A quiet, humble spirit is of great worth in God's sight. No amount of money can buy it.

Lord God, please guide me to see beyond appearances and into the hearts of others. I deeply respect those who quietly serve You while seeking no recognition for their work.

Christ in All of Us

There is no difference in men in this new life. Greeks and Jews are the same. . . . There is no difference between nations. Men who are servants and those who are free are the same. Christ is everything. He is in all of us.

COLOSSIANS 3:11

In 2024, the number of Christians in the world exceeded 2.5 billion.[39] Christians live in every nation. They speak many different languages and are part of many different ethnic cultures. Some Christians are free, and others are restrained by their governments. Some are rich; others are poor. There are Christians who live in mansions and those who are grateful to have a roof over their heads. Some are homeless. But there is one thing all Christians have in common: They believe in Jesus. The Bible says that God does not respect one person more than another (Acts 10:34). All are welcome in His kingdom, regardless of their race, nationality, or ethnicity. The only requirement is inviting Jesus into their hearts.

God loves all Christians equally no matter their social status or the place they live. Whether they are well-dressed or in dirty jeans, whether they are short, tall, overweight, or slim, God loves and accepts them all, and He encourages us to do the same.

Father God, help me to look beyond our differences and remember that all Christians are members of Your family. We are sisters and brothers in Christ.

The Error of Our Ways

These things show us something. They teach us not to want things that are bad for us like those people did.

1 CORINTHIANS 10:6

As parents, we reprimand our children when they knowingly do something wrong. We say, "You know better than that." Our children aren't perfect. But neither are we. All of us have done what we know is wrong, whether something as trivial as getting a parking ticket or something bigger that caused us shame.

When we read the Bible, we see many examples of good people who chose to do wrong. David had an adulterous relationship with Bathsheba, who became pregnant with his child. Jonah refused to follow God's instructions and ran from Him. Peter told Jesus he would never leave Him and then, three times, denied knowing Him. Whether it was to satisfy their own desires or because they were overwhelmed by fear, God's people knowingly did what was wrong. We can learn from their mistakes not to want things that are bad for us, and we can learn something else: When we are aware of what's right but choose wrong, we can still be reconciled with God. David, Jonah, and Peter all repented of their sins, and God forgave them. If we pray and repent, we can be certain that God will forgive us as well.

Lord, I know what I did was wrong, and I'm sorry. Please forgive me.

Lady in Waiting

Dear friends, remember this one thing, with the Lord one day is as 1,000 years, and 1,000 years are as one day.
2 PETER 3:8

Robin prayed, "God, we're being patient, but please hurry." Robin and her husband had been married for a year. When they married, they planned to have a child right away. But that hadn't happened. Robin's patience had all but run out. When she prayed asking God to hurry, she felt a twinge of guilt. After all, who was she to ask the Creator of the universe to hurry! Then one day, while reading the psalms, Robin discovered someone else who prayed asking God to hurry: King David. "Hurry to help me!" he begged (Psalm 22:19; 38:22). "O my God, do not wait" (40:17). Throughout the book of Psalms, Robin found David crying out to God, "Please hurry!" and as she read, she noticed that God always brought David through his times of worry and trouble.

We tend to hold God to our way of measuring time, forgetting that His timing is always perfect. He hears us when we pray, and He will reward our patience. Robin continued to pray, asking God to give her and her husband a child, but she left the outcome to His timing. She knew that God had heard her prayers, and she would wait patiently for His answer.

Dear God, grant me the patience to pray for and trust in Your perfect timing.

Increase My Faith

"Lord, I have faith. Help my weak faith to be stronger!"
Mark 9:24

We have faith that what we see exists, but faith in the Lord we find more challenging. Perhaps because we can't see Him, it's hard to trust Jesus completely. Even His disciples who *could* see Him found it difficult.

The disciples were in a boat on the lake before daylight when they saw a figure walking toward them on the water. They were afraid. "At once Jesus spoke to them and said, 'Take hope. It is I. Do not be afraid!' Peter said to Jesus, 'If it is You, Lord, tell me to come to You on the water.' Jesus said, 'Come!' Peter got out of the boat and walked on the water to Jesus. But when he saw the strong wind, he was afraid. He began to go down in the water. He cried out, 'Lord, save me!' At once Jesus put out His hand and took hold of him. Jesus said to Peter, 'You have so little faith! Why did you doubt?'" (Matthew 14:27–31).

The Bible says, "Without faith it is impossible to please God, because anyone who comes to him must believe that he exists" (Hebrews 11:6 NIV). We all have moments when our faith is weak and we wonder if our Lord is real. Hebrews 11:1 tells us, "Faith. . . is being sure of what we cannot see." Ask Jesus today for increased faith so you can entrust your life to Him.

Jesus, I want to trust You completely.
Please strengthen my faith.

Our Father, the Architect

Commit to the Lord *whatever you do,*
and he will establish your plans.
Proverbs 16:3 NIV

Holly and her husband, Tad, met with their architect regarding plans for their new home. Their list of needs and wants was long. Holly doubted the architect had fit everything they asked for into 1,700 square feet. But as she and Tad studied the blueprint, Holly was pleasantly surprised. The architect had given them not just what they wanted but more. By combining creativity with his technical skills, he had designed a home for Holly and Tad that was both pleasing and functional.

Hebrews 3:4 tells us, "Every house is built by someone. And God is the One Who has built everything." If our architects on earth can create plans that exceed our expectations, imagine what God, the architect of the universe, can do. His skills and creativity are infinite. There isn't a problem He can't solve. When we commit our hopes and dreams to Him, God will establish our plans. Expect that it will be an ongoing process. Along the way, there will be changes, improvements, and modifications; above all, we'll be responsible for working to implement God's plans alongside Him. His blueprint might not be how we envisioned it—it will be even better!

Lord God, I commit my hopes and dreams to You. I thank You that Your plans for me are exceedingly more abundant than I can imagine.

My Stars

He knows the number of the stars.
He gives names to all of them.
PSALM 147:4

In *The Little Prince* by Antoine de Saint-Exupéry, the prince says that all people view the stars differently—to each, they mean something different. Some see the stars as guides. . .others see them as nothing more than little lights. . . . Essentially, the stars hold unique significance for individuals, according to what is most important in their lives.

Blessed are those who look at the stars and see them as God's handiwork. They look up with wonder that He puts all the stars in their places, knows how many there are, and gives each a name. For those who love God, the stars are not silent. They speak God's name, praising Him. Isaiah says, "Lift up your eyes and see. Who has made these stars?. . . Because of the greatness of His strength, and because He is strong in power, not one of them is missing" (Isaiah 40:26).

How do you see the stars? Are they more than little lights in the sky? If you look up and beyond them, you will discover the one who holds you in the palm of His hand.

Father God, the stars tell me of Your glory.
They shine the light of Your love down
upon me and give me peace.

Centered on Love

Love from the center of who you are; don't fake it.
ROMANS 12:9 MSG

In Sunday school, little Susan learned that God fills our hearts to overflowing with His love and that He wants us to share what's left over. Susan talked with her mother about how she could share God's love with their neighbors. She and her mother baked cookies and put them into gift bags. Susan made cards to go with the bags, personalizing each one: "God loves you, Mrs. Nelson. I hope you feel better soon!" "Your yard looks great, Mr. Hobbes. God loves you!" . . . The little girl's compassion, caring, and kindness were evident when she delivered her gifts to each recipient. Young children have a simple and straightforward relationship with God. They accept what He says at face value. They act upon His words, and they love from the center of their hearts.

As adults, things like worry, anger, judgment, and stubbornness can crowd and even evict God's love from our hearts. But if we dismiss those things and allow God to be at the center of our being, He will release in us a rushing river of love, more than we can contain. So let love pour out from you today. When you do, you will be reflecting the heart of God.

Dear God, may Your love flow through me and result in overflowing acts of compassion, kindness, forgiveness, and peace.

Sour Grapes

Catch for us the foxes, the little foxes that ruin the vineyards.
SONG OF SOLOMON 2:15 NIV

You might remember reading some of Aesop's fables. Although there is uncertainty about whether Aesop truly existed, he is credited with writing a vast collection of fables that each end with a moral, or lesson. One of the most well-known is "The Fox and the Grapes." A hungry fox desires a bunch of ripe, juicy grapes hanging on a vine beyond his reach. With all his might, he jumps as high as he can, trying to reach them. Again and again, he fails. The fox finally gives up and walks away, saying, "I don't need your sour grapes. They aren't even ripe yet!" The moral of the story is: There are many who despise what they can't reach.[40]

Those who are jealous and resent others for their accomplishments are like little foxes that ruin vineyards. They nibble at the character of good people. In the Bible James wrote, "Wherever you find jealousy and fighting, there will be trouble and every other kind of wrong-doing" (James 3:16). We should be careful not to allow covetousness to slip into our hearts. It pulls us away from our loving God who supplies all our needs.

Oh Lord, save me from envy and greedy desires. Help me to keep my eyes fixed on You and Your generous blessings. Thank You for providing all that I need.

A Little Bit of Heaven

The Spirit of God whets our appetite by giving us a taste of what's ahead. He puts a little of heaven in our hearts so that we'll never settle for less.

2 CORINTHIANS 5:5 MSG

What if, instead of focusing on the world's troubles, the media focused on the wonders of nature, the sunrise igniting the gray morning sky, minerals sparkling on a sandy beach, the sunset melting into dusk, meteor showers exploding in the sky. . . Imagine every news story centering on people loving one another through acts of compassion, caring, and kindness. That world only exists in our imaginations, but God scatters little hints of heaven all around us to remind us of what's ahead.

Dictionaries define the noun *wonder* as something causing a feeling of surprise, excitement, or amazement. The verb *wonder* means to be curious about something. Wonder is all around us. Little bits of heaven are found in nature, the people we meet, sounds we hear, scents we smell, sights we see, and things we taste. They make us wonder about the enormity of God and His ability to control and create. They lead us to imagine what heaven is like. Today, focus on the little bits of heaven all around you. Then think about how much is left unseen.

Oh the wonder of it all, Lord! Thank You for a little bit of heaven right here on earth.

No Greater Love

"No one can have greater love than to give his life for his friends."
JOHN 15:13

Almost every day we hear stories of heroes who gave their lives to save others. In Wisconsin, an off-duty police officer died saving a restaurant employee during an armed robbery. A father in North Carolina drowned while saving his sons who had fallen into a river. These are sad stories, but also a testament to all those who have given their lives in exchange for another. These heroic men and women modeled the attitude of Christ, who, because of His deep love for us, selflessly gave His life to save ours. Christ's love working through these heroes put fear out of their hearts (1 John 4:18). Out of love, they willingly made the lives of others more important than their own.

Selfless acts don't always end in death. We give up a little of our own lives each time we sacrifice our wants for the needs of others. We quit our jobs to care for a dying parent, give up our dreams to help our children realize theirs, donate money, and even donate blood and organs as acts of selfless love. Each selfless act reflects the love of God inside our hearts. Nothing is greater or more satisfying than sharing His love with others.

Heavenly Father, help me to love selflessly and willingly, putting the needs of others before my own.

Angels Watch Over Me

For He will tell His angels to care for
you and keep you in all your ways.
PSALM 91:11

Angels. They are sometimes called the "heavenly hosts" or the "armies of heaven." God created angels as spirits that are almost always invisible to humans. The Bible, however, tells of people who saw angels. Abraham, Gideon, Zechariah, Mary, the shepherds in fields near Bethlehem. . .all of them were visited by angels they could see. The Bible names just two angels, Michael and Gabriel. We don't know how many others exist, but in Revelation 5:11 (NIV) John says there are "thousands upon thousands." Psalm 103:20 says that God's angels do whatever He commands, and Zechariah 1:10–11 suggests God's angels roam the earth. God's angels are more powerful than humans, and they battle Satan's forces. And the Bible is clear that God sends His angels to protect us.

Think about it—not only does God Himself watch over and protect us, but He gives us extra layers of protection: His Son, Jesus; the Holy Spirit; and a whole army of angels. So when you feel lonely or afraid, be encouraged! Angels watch over you. You are surrounded by love, and you are never alone.

Father God, thank You for Your mighty power and for the angels who watch over me. Thank You for layers of protection that make me feel safe and give me peace.

False Prophets

Only the L*ORD gives wisdom;*
he gives knowledge and understanding.
PROVERBS 2:6 NCV

The French get credit for inventing the fortune-telling game "*effeuiller la marguerite*."[41] We know it as "He Loves Me, He Loves Me Not." Petals are picked off a daisy, and the last petal reveals the answer. Games and superstitions like this one have been around for centuries. The prophet Isaiah warned against believing in such things. He said, "Some people say, 'Ask the mediums and fortune-tellers, who whisper and mutter, what to do.' But I tell you that people should ask their God for help" (Isaiah 8:19 NCV).

God is the source of all wisdom. He has all the answers. We don't need to consult fortune-tellers or mediums to determine what the future holds. God is the only one who knows the plan for our lives. If we are uncertain about something, we should ask Him. He knows exactly what we should do. When we bring our thoughts and questions to God in prayer, He gives us knowledge and understanding. The Bible warns against trusting false prophets. Paul says in 2 Corinthians 11:13–14, "They make themselves look like true missionaries of Christ. It is no surprise! The devil makes himself look like an angel of light."

Heavenly Father, keep me away from false prophets.
I will trust You as the only one with perfect answers.
You are the source of all wisdom and truth.

Guard Your Heart

Above all else, guard your heart,
for everything you do flows from it.
PROVERBS 4:23 NIV

At a luncheon honoring centenarians, each was asked to reveal their secret for living a long life. Some credited the food they ate, love of family and friends, hard work, sports, fitness, and hobbies, but when Edna gave her answer, she quoted Proverbs 4:23. "Above all else, guard your heart, for everything you do flows from it." When she was a young woman, Edna had fallen into sin. She'd made many mistakes. But in her late forties, Edna met a woman who led her to Christ. Edna's life was never the same. Instead of sin flowing into her heart, Edna's heart was filled to overflowing with God's goodness. From that day on, Edna did her best to share His goodness with everyone she met.

When we consciously work at guarding our hearts from sin, we stay focused on pleasing God. The more we desire to please Him, the more we learn about how much He loves us. We come to understand His power to guide, help, correct, and forgive us, and we learn to trust Him for strength, comfort, protection, and peace. When you pray, ask God to fill your heart as He did Edna's—overflowing with His goodness and love.

Oh Lord, help me to keep sin from entering my heart. Be my shield. Let Your almighty power strengthen me against Satan's tricks and lies.

Always and Forever

"For I, the Lord, do not change."
MALACHI 3:6

Although the Bible has been translated into many different languages, the truth of God's Word remains the same. The essence of its many stories hasn't changed. The messages God gave to the prophets haven't changed. Neither have God's commands and instructions about how we should live. God's plan for the world hasn't changed either. Every plan, every promise, remains exactly as it was in the beginning.

The American philosopher Henry David Thoreau thought deeply and analyzed his thoughts. Although sometimes critical of Christianity, much of what Thoreau wrote aligned with the truths in God's Word. For example, "Things do not change; we change."[42] God created us to adapt to all the changes happening around and within us. Nothing happens outside His knowledge and control.

The only thing that won't change is God. His sovereignty is the same today as it always has been. He will not change in His character or change His plans. We can trust every promise in the Bible to be fulfilled, and we can trust God to love us forever and guide us throughout our lives. In this ever-changing world, isn't it a comfort to know that God and His loving-kindness will last forever?

Heavenly Father, whenever I feel overwhelmed by the changes that surround me, I come to You for comfort. You are my solid ground in this tangled, chaotic world.

Straight from Heaven

Then the angel showed me the river of the water of life. It was as clear as glass and came from the throne of God and of the Lamb.
REVELATION 22:1

A river's source is the place it begins. It might be an underground spring or lake, small streams in the mountains, even a melting glacier. Every river has a source. The Bible tells us that Jesus is the source of living water. The book of Revelation reveals even more. In a vision, John saw the river of the water of life in heaven. Its source was God's throne. We can imagine this river coming down to us from heaven, flowing through Jesus into our hearts, and filling us with the truth of God's Word.

The river of the water of life is ever flowing. It will never run dry. It is always clear and fresh. If we drink from it, it not only refreshes us but also renews our strength and gives us hope. Resting beside the river, we find comfort and peace. Jesus is there talking with us, counseling us, and guiding us through this journey called life. And when our bodies die, we can imagine our souls being carried by the river back to its heavenly source. The river of the water of life is a beautiful symbol of God's infinite and everlasting love.

Lord, lead me to the river of the water of life. Refresh and restore my soul.

The Alpha and Omega

I am Alpha and Omega, the beginning and the end.
REVELATION 21:6 KJV

Alpha and omega are the first and last letters of the Greek alphabet. In the Bible, these words symbolize God the Father and Jesus the Son. They remind us that God and Jesus are infinite.

Jesus was with God in the beginning (John 1:1) and He will be with God in the end. In Revelation 1:8 Jesus says, "I am the All-powerful One Who was and Who is and Who is to come." Jesus is coming to earth again to judge all mankind and to take those who trust in Him to be with Him forever (Luke 21:25–28). Until that day, Jesus offers us the gift of living water. It is free and freely given. It is the gift of salvation that comes when we confess our sins to Jesus and invite Him into our hearts. It is the one and only act that allows the river of the water of life to flow into us from heaven. Jesus told us that no one knows when He will come again. It could be today or years or even centuries from now. But since we don't know, it is paramount that we ask Him into our hearts so we can live our lives in peace and look forward to heaven.

Dear God, may we all resonate with the Bible's last words: "'Yes, I am coming soon!' Let it be so. Come, Lord Jesus" (Revelation 22:20). May Your people experience the loving-favor of the Lord Jesus Christ.

Beautiful Feet

How beautiful are the feet of them that preach the gospel of peace, and bring glad tidings of good things!

ROMANS 10:15 KJV

Aren't pedicures wonderful? How relaxing it is to soak our tired feet and have someone massage them. How fun it is to pick out nail polish and maybe even some embellishments. We leave the salon with beautiful feet that make us feel pretty.

The Bible tells of another kind of beautiful feet. (Spoiler alert: They aren't always pretty.) They are the feet of those who bring the good news that Jesus saves us from sin. They are the feet of those who tell of God's power, protection, goodness, and love. These are the feet of Jesus' disciples who are willing to walk through the earth's mud and muck to share God's Word with others. In God's sight, these are beautiful feet.

We were made to share the gospel of Christ. God created us to be modern-day disciples with the mission of leading others to accept His gift of living water. Maybe you know people who are thirsty and need Jesus to come into their hearts. Stand on your beautiful feet and start walking. Bring them the news of peace, gladness, and everything good.

Dear Jesus, teach me to guide others to put their hope and trust in You. Please lead them to accept Your gift of living water and eternal life in Your presence. Amen.

Scripture Index

OLD TESTAMENT

NEW TESTAMENT

Endnotes

1. See the Kavik River Camp website at http://www.kavikrivercamp.com/index.html. See also David Strege, "Living 'Life Below Zero' at Kavik River Camp," *Men's Journal,* October 8, 2021, https://www.mensjournal.com/adventure/living-life-below-zero-at-kavik-river-camp-alaska.

2. Merriam-Webster.com Dictionary, s.v. "craving," accessed August 24, 2024, https://www.merriam-webster.com/dictionary/craving.

3. Cambridge Advanced Learner's Dictionary and Thesaurus, s.v. "doom monger," accessed August 24, 2024, https://dictionary.cambridge.org/us/dictionary/english/doom-monger.

4. Samantha Vincenty, "Debbie Downer: A History of Rachel Dratch's Iconic SNL Character," NBC.com, August 24, 2023, https://www.nbc.com/nbc-insider/debbie-downer-origin-snl-rachel-dratch.

5. https://www.google.com/books/edition/Biblical_Ethics_The_Moral_Foundations_of/g86WCgAAQBAJ?hl=en&gbpv=1&dq=%22Certain+things+can+only+be+dealt+with%22+oswald+chambers&pg=PT69&printsec=frontcover.

6. "It Is Well with My Soul," Blue Letter Bible, accessed August 24, 2024, https://www.blueletterbible.org/hymns/i/It_Is_Well_With_My_Soul.cfm. For more information, see Chris Fenner with Chuck Bumgardner, "It Is Well with My Soul," Hymnology Archive, July 5, 2018, https://www.hymnologyarchive.com/it-is-well-with-my-soul.

7. "Baker, Ray Stannard [David Grayson] (1870–1946)," Wisconsin Historical Society, accessed August 24, 2024, https://www.wisconsinhistory.org/Records/Article/CS1654.

8. David Grayson, *The Friendly Road: New Adventures in Contentment* (Doubleday, Page & Co., 1913), https://www.gutenberg.org/files/2479/2479-h/2479-h.htm.

9. Zora Neale Hurston, *Their Eyes Were Watching God* (Lippincott, 1937), 21, https://pressbooks.library.torontomu.ca/theireyeswerewatchinggod/chapter/3/.

10. *Quoted in Alexandra Hurtado, "Celebrate Roald Dahl Day with 70 of the Author's Most Memorable Quotes," Parade, November 23, 2022, #37, https://parade.com/1087241/alexandra-hurtado/roald-dahl-quotes/.

11. Quoted in Elizabeth Drake, "Roald Dahl: 10 Quotes on His Birthday," Christian Science Monitor, September 13, 2012, https://www.csmonitor.com/Books/2012/0913/Roald-Dahl-10-quotes-on-his-birthday/Good-thoughts.

12. Collins COBUILD Advanced Learner's Dictionary, s.v. "at any price," accessed August 24, 2024, https://www.collinsdictionary.com/us/dictionary/english/at-any-price.

13. https://caga.org/the-trail/garden-areas/.

14. Quoted in "Salvation Quotes: 20 of the Best Book Quotes About Salvation," **Bookroo,** accessed August 24, 2024, https://bookroo.com/quotes/salvation.

15. "About Us," Red Hat Society, accessed August 24, 2024, https://redhatsociety.com/about-us/.

16. William Shakespeare, *The Taming of the Shrew,* lines 82–83, Folger Shakespeare Library, https://www.folger.edu/explore/shakespeares-works/the-taming-of-the-shrew/read/.

17. Joseph M. Scriven, "What a Friend We Have in Jesus" (1855), https://hymnary.org/text/what_a_friend_we_have_in_jesus_all_our_s.

18. Jay Macpherson, "Scriven, Joseph Medlicott," in *Dictionary of Canadian Biography,* vol. 11, University of Toronto/Université Laval, 2003–, accessed August 24, 2024, https://www.biographi.ca/en/bio/scriven_joseph_medlicott_11E.html.

19. "Twice the Pride," *Star Wars*, accessed August 24, 2024, https://www.starwars.com/video/twice-the-pride.

20. https://azquotes.com/quote/766517

21. Quoted in Jeff Robinson, "God Moves in a Mysterious Way," *The Gospel Coalition,* April 24, 2015, https://www.thegospelcoalition.org/article/god-moves-in-a-mysterious-way/.

22. Quoted in John Piper, "Insanity and Spiritual Songs in the Soul of a Saint: Reflections on the Life of William Cowper," *Desiring God,* January 29, 1992, https://www.desiringgod.org/messages/insanity-and-spiritual-songs-in-the-soul-of-a-saint. See also "William Cowper," Hymnary.org, accessed August 24, 2024, https://hymnary.org/person/Cowper_W.

23. Quoted in "Laugh," Presidential Prayer Team, April 10, 2020, https://www.presidentialprayerteam.org/2020/04/10/laugh/.

24. Mayo Clinic Staff, "Stress Relief from Laughter? It's No Joke," Mayo Clinic, September 22, 2023, https://www.mayoclinic.org/healthy-lifestyle/stress-management/in-depth/stress-relief/art-20044456.

25. Quoted in Daniel Blake, "Gabby Douglas Praises God; Christian Gymnast Thankful After Winning All-Around Gold at Olympics 2012," *Christian Post,* August 2, 2012, https://www.christianpost.com/news/gabby-douglas-praises-god-christian-gymnast-thankful-after-winning-all-around-gold-at-olympics-2012.html.

26. Meghan Jones, "The 23 Hardest Winning Words from the National Spelling Bee," *Reader's Digest,* June 2, 2023, https://www.rd.com/list/winning-spelling-bee-words/.

27. "Dust in the Wind," written by Kelly Livgren, from the album *Point of Know Return* (Sony/ATV Music Publishing, 1977), https://www.songfacts.com/lyrics/kansas/dust-in-the-wind.

28. "Meet Candace," Candace Lightner, accessed August 24, 2024, https://www.candacelightner.com/Meet-Candace/Biography.

29. Luther F. Beecher, "What Is Dying?" *Northwest Christian Advocate*, July 13, 1904. Public domain.

30. Quoted in Tyler Huckabee, "11 Mr. Rogers Quotes Every Christian Should Read," *Relevant*, November 22, 2019, https://relevantmagazine.com/culture/10-mr-rogers-quotes-you-need-read/.

31. "'Angel Wings,' Rainbows for Michalski Procession," WTMJ News, January 4, 2019, https://wtmj.com/news/2019/01/04/angel-wings-rainbows-for-michalski-procession/.

32. See Chris Fenner, "In the Garden," Hymnology Archive, September 18, 2019, https://www.hymnologyarchive.com/in-the-garden.

33. Merriam-Webster.com Dictionary, s.v. "believe," accessed August 24, 2024, https://www.merriam-webster.com/dictionary/believe.

34. Merriam-Webster.com Dictionary, s.v. "believe in," accessed August 24, 2024, https://www.merriam-webster.com/dictionary/believe%20in.

35. See Rachel Brodsky, "Helen Reddy's 'I Am Woman': The Story Behind the Song," uDiscoverMusic, May 1, 2024, https://www.udiscovermusic.com/stories/helen-reddy-i-am-woman-song-feature/.

36. Bill O'Brian, "Eagles Across America," U.S. Fish & Wildlife Service, January 13, 2023, https://www.fws.gov/story/eagles-across-america.

37. "Historical Quotes," plainlanguage.gov, accessed August 24, 2024, https://www.plainlanguage.gov/resources/quotes/historical-quotes/.

38. Don Seitz, *Artemus Ward: A Biography and Bibliography*, p. 113-114 (New York: Harper & Brothers, 1919; New York: Beekman, 1974).

39. "Global Christianity Surges Beyond Projections in 2024," LiCAS.news, February 9, 2024, https://www.licas.news/2024/02/09/global-christianity-surges-beyond-projections-in-2024/.

40. "The Fox and the Grapes," Wikipedia, accessed August 24, 2024, https://en.wikipedia.org/wiki/The_Fox_and_the_Grapes.

41. "He Loves Me. . .He Loves Me Not Facts for Kids," Kiddle, October 16, 2023, https://kids.kiddle.co/He_loves_me..._he_loves_me_not.

42. "Henry David Thoreau: Walden," The Literature Page, accessed August 24, 2024, http://www.literaturepage.com/read/walden-247.html.